Expressions From Surrey

Edited by Allison Jones

First published in Great Britain in 2010 by

Remus House
Coltsfoot Drive
Peterborough
PE2 9JX
Telephone: 01733 890066
Website: www.youngwriters.co.uk

Book Design by Spencer Hart

SB ISBN 978-1-84924-844-0

Foreword

At Young Writers our defining aim is to promote an enjoyment of reading and writing amongst children and young adults. By giving aspiring poets the opportunity to see their work in print, their love of the written word as well as confidence in their own abilities has the chance to blossom.

Our latest competition Poetry Explorers was designed to introduce primary school children to the wonders of creative expression. They were given free reign to write on any theme and in any style, thus encouraging them to use and explore a variety of different poetic forms.

We are proud to present the resulting collection of regional anthologies which are an excellent showcase of young writing talent. With such a diverse range of entries received, the selection process was difficult yet very rewarding. From comical rhymes to poignant verses, there is plenty to entertain and inspire within these pages. We hope you agree that this collection bursting with imagination is one to treasure.

Contents

Purley Oaks Primary School

Whyteleafe Primary School

Woodlea Primary School

Worplesdon Primary School

The Poems

Autumn Days

The air smells cleaner,
The days shorten,
The days darken,
The grass gets greener,
The sky turns black,
The clocks go back,
The clouds change,
And the air exchanges,
Does autumn change?

Natasha Fearon (11)

Volcanoes

The rumbling shook the earth with anxiety,
The indignant volcano rose from its depth,
Soon to spread its hidden wrath.

Ghostly, the moon tiptoes around the cold volcano,
Certain to infuriate the land with its icy fire.

Chante McLaughlin (11)

Poppies

I am a deep, deep red poppy
In a dirty, muddy battlefield,
I'm upset all the soldiers are
Standing on me.
An injured soldier is trampling on me
Bleeding to death,
A heavy soldier is crushing me
And also squashing me.
He's in a green,
Hard uniform filled
With red, squishy
Blood!

Kimberley Willington (10)
Amy Johnson Primary School

I Don't Want To Be A Gun

I don't want to be a gun,
I want to be a shiny bike
So children can ride me and be happy.

I don't want to be a gun
I want to be a dark red toy car
So children can play happily with me.

I don't want to be a gun
I want a dark green helmet
So I can protect a soldier from getting hit in the head.

I don't want to be a gun
I want to be a golden locket
So I can keep long-time memories.

I don't want to be a gun
I don't want to be a killer!

Rebecca Dorey (10)
Amy Johnson Primary School

Poppies Of War

P oppies are red, red remembrance
O ver the Flanders fields, fields of blood
P oppies remember November the eleventh
P oppies are flowers, flowers of war
'I might be the colour of blood but I'm not a killer,' said a poppy
E ndless of war and remembrance blood
S aved lives and gone lives

O ver Flanders field
F or the bloody petals of poppies

W e together wonder what is it like.
A ll together we shall
R emember the eleventh of November.

Mahreen Mousoof (11)
Amy Johnson Primary School

Poppies In War

Poppies are flowers,
Poppies are bloodshed,
Poppies are flowers,
Poppies are soldiers,
Guns and bombs,
Poppies are flowers,
Flowers in war,
But they're no killers.

Poppies are red,
Poppies are black,
Poppies are red,
Poppies are green,
Poppies are red,
Red as blood,
But there are no victims.

Rou Egremont (10)
Amy Johnson Primary School

Poppies

I want to give up being a poppy,
I've been a poppy too long.

I want to be a bright sunflower,
Shining in someone's lush, green garden.

I want to give up being a poppy,
I've been a poppy too long.

I want to be some perfume, or a rose bush
So pretty.

The question is;
Can you give up being a blood supporter?

Leah Turner (10)
Amy Johnson Primary School

Battlefield

I used to be a colourful carnival,
So lively and funny,
The dust cloud ground gathered lots of people to
My welcoming carnival.
But now I'm feeling pain upon my heavy head,
I feel so empty I'm going to cry,
Because I'm a horrible nasty battlefield!
I also feel I'm so dead but it looks like I've already died,
So now I'm not noticed.
I might as well live with it.
Hope for me that I will soon change back again.

Courteney Cox (11)
Amy Johnson Primary School

Poppies

Soldiers are poppies,
Their bodies covered in blood,
Fighting, dying,
Trying to help the world.

Poppies, bloodshed,
Hiding in trenches,
Holes in their chests,
Bullets in the head.

Poppies, poppies, worn in different countries,
Wear one for the soldiers.

Marisa Davey (11)
Amy Johnson Primary School

The Sound Of Gunfire

The sound of gunfire
Travelling in the breeze.

The sound of young men crying as they lay upon
The thick, dirty mud.

The smell of people's torment drifting
Up my nostrils.

I want to be snuggled in my mother's arms,
Sipping a hot cup of tea.

That's what I want.

Kody Emberson (11)
Amy Johnson Primary School

Bullet

I used to be a lucky coin, beautiful
Gold and round.
They melted, pressed and shaped me into
A bullet.
I was given to a soldier to take someone's
Life.
The soldier put me into the gun barrel.
He fired me.
I took a life, killed a man.
I want to be a coin again.

Louis Wilkinson (11)
Amy Johnson Primary School

Battlefield

I used to be a garden,
So beautiful and attractive,
My tall, luscious, emerald green grass,
The audience to the drifting but melodic birds.
But not for long
Now I'm the hearer of pain and I can feel the colour of death.
Gunshots in my ear,
Footsteps on my belly
And raindrops falling silently in my mouth.
Now I'm a soggy, wet and muddy battlefield!

Callum Stalley (11)
Amy Johnson Primary School

I Am Death

I wish I was with my family,
Warm and clean and not smothered in blood
Instead I'm in the battlefield
Killing for my country.
I can hear crashing of the bombs crashing on the ground.
I do nothing
I have no family for now I'm dead
I killed so many people that
Now I'm *death!*

Shannon Louise White (10)
Amy Johnson Primary School

The Bomb

I used to be a bouncy ball,
I got bounced round the house
I miss my colours pink, blue and black
And I can't get them back
Because I'm a *bomb!*

Kayleigh Dennis (10)
Amy Johnson Primary School

The Bomb

I used to be colourful, beautiful,
And sweet.
Swaying side to side in the gorgeous wind,
Being picked for nice occasions.
But now I see bombs being dropped onto houses,
Battlefields killing people.
I don't want to see people getting killed,
I want children to pick me,
And to be put in gorgeous houses.

Maryon Craven (10)
Amy Johnson Primary School

Give Up Being A Poppy

I want to give up being a poppy.
But neither do I want to be a gun or a bomb.
I give up with these things.

I would rather be a horse in a green, lovely field
Doing nothing but eating grass.

I want to be a pocket watch
In the hands of a brave true mother.
To speed up the time until her husband or son comes home.

Mohammed Mbarak (11)
Amy Johnson Primary School

Battlefield

I used to be a lively theme park,
So energetic and free,
The rides all brought fun and laughter too everything I could see,
But everything has changed now – sights, sounds,
Fun and laughter, it's not so lively and not so fun
It's just a dull grey field,
But in the distance you can hear the sound of
A gun going off then a man screaming with pain.

Louise Charlotte Sales (11)
Amy Johnson Primary School

Anderson Shelter

I am an Anderson shelter
I protect my family

I am a mother shielding my children
Last Sunday another shelter got bombed
I felt the vibration from the earth

But I stand tall
Protecting my family.

George Wallis (10)
Amy Johnson Primary School

Dreams

When I go to sleep
I dream of lovely things
Everything I dream about
Is sweet and kind and gleams

When I wake up
I think of my dreams
When I think about them
It makes me beam.

Isabelle Costello (6)
Corpus Christi Catholic Primary School

My Family

My family is cool!
My family rules!

My brother's called Cole,
He likes to rock 'n' roll!

My mum is called Sarah
She's a good carer!

My dad is called Nick,
He isn't very quick!

My dog is called Fred,
He likes to go to bed!

My gerbils are called Goldy and Jack,
They're both quite fat!

My nan is called Angie,
Trampolining, can she?

My grandad's called John,
Awww, he's gone.

My uncle's called Paul,
He is very tall.

My auntie is called Nicki,
She likes the mouse called Mickey.

My cousins are Hazel and James,
They are not a pain!

My family is cool!
My family rules!

Gina Angelica Dearson Adams (9)
Corpus Christi Catholic Primary School

Pumpkin Pie

I was eating pumpkin pie
Then over came Elliott to say hi
We then looked up to the sky
'That's funny,' I said, 'Where are the stars?
All I can see are bars.'
Then I realised I was inside
She was playing her new game
The game was called Fame
It showed the name of the stars
Up in the bars.
I decided to have a go
The game was boring though
Then I went to say hi to my pumpkin pie
Sadly it was gone
Then I saw Kirsty complain she was thirsty
I then realised she had eaten my pie
She was going to die,
I complained about Kirsty
She then started to cry
Then I had *her* pumpkin pie!

Oliver Costello (11)
Corpus Christi Catholic Primary School

My Lovely Kitten

One day my mummy brought me a small kitten.
It was a girl. She was so cute.
She had an orange star on her forehead.
She was very cheeky.
She was very interested in everything
Because she was sniffing around with her black cute nose.
I gave her a name, Elze, because I had a similar kitten in Lithuania.
Now my kitten is about fifteen weeks old.
She is growing up very fast because she drinks a lot of milk.
I love my kitten.

Auksé Linkeviciute (7)
Corpus Christi Catholic Primary School

My Stuff Is Being Eaten!

I see a door, I see a dinosaur,
The dinosaur eats the door,
Then he smiles at me!

I see a flower pot, I see a monster,
The monster eats the flower pot,
Then he winks at me!

I see a chair, I see a dragon,
The dragon eats the chair,
Then he grins at me!

I see a lamp, I see a sea monster,
The sea monster eats the lamp,
Then he says, *'I'm still hungry!'*
And then he eats *me!*

Lucie Cozens (8)
Corpus Christi Catholic Primary School

Dear Teacher

Another school year has truly begun
But please we still want to have more fun!
We want to play hide-and-seek
And pretend to be Laserbeak.
Ben 10 is our coolest hero
But not the eighty minus eighty equals zero.
Crazy bones 4 are the latest to have
But you ask us to go early to bed!
We want to play Nintendo DS
And not to have another spelling test.
Kicking football is our game
And not knowing legends should not be a shame.
Please let us be young and carefree
For as long as we want to be.

Simon Raymond (8)
Corpus Christi Catholic Primary School

Water

Water, water everywhere,
On the ground and in the air.
It falls as raindrops from the sky,
As a river flowing by.

A solid form is called ice,
In my drink is very nice.
Another form is called steam,
From a kettle it is seen.

Water is used by you and me,
Washing, cleaning, cups of tea.
Water can be used for fun.
Swimming, sailing, a water gun!

Michelle Hazell (9)
Corpus Christi Catholic Primary School

Waterfall

W ater pure to drink
A s good as gold
T ears run down your cheeks
E choes of the stream
R ivers flowing fast and slow
F alling, falling from up high
A gain falling, falling from up high
L apping the shores
L apping, lapping, lapping.

Isabella Pederzolli (9)
Corpus Christi Catholic Primary School

Water

Water, water everywhere,
Come here, go there
Water you are nice for me to drink,
Water you are fun for me to play with.

Water you are sometimes dangerous,
Water you are blue,
Water you are cool,
Water you are amazing when you turn into ice.

Tharushi Denipitya (9)
Corpus Christi Catholic Primary School

Elephants And Mice

Elephants and mice are big and small
Elephants and mice are short and tall
The mouse makes a very quiet noise
But the elephant's noise will blow away some boys!
Elephants live in zoos where people come to clap and cheer,
Mice live in holes and try to steal our cheese and beer.
Elephants eat lots of food, mice don't eat as much
But both are cuter than a rabbit in a hutch!

Isabelle Foot (9)
Corpus Christi Catholic Primary School

Volcano

V iolent explosion deep in the earth
O n my tongue I can taste ash that blocks my lungs
L oud crackles sizzling down the mountain
C raters brimming with hot lava
A warning's sent out, animals start to run
N ow all the mountain top explodes
O range flames light the sky!

Tessa King (7)
Corpus Christi Catholic Primary School

Sunshine

Sunshine is bright,
Isn't in the night
But is always there at day.
Shining our way,
For every boy and girl.
It's a dazzling curl
Of sparkling light
And is always a sight!

Hakyung Lee (10)
Corpus Christi Catholic Primary School

My Beautiful Waterfall

Water source from high above,
Colour everywhere shadow from my waterfall rough and tumble,
When you hear a grumble and the water starts to flow.
My waterfall so beautiful against the sun,
A chilly breeze flies through my hair as the water comes from high to low.
It's such a show
Better than the cinema, my beautiful waterfall.

Fleur Swindle (10)
Corpus Christi Catholic Primary School

Autumn Time

Autumn, autumn, very cold.
Lots of colours, bright and bold.
Rainy days horrible and wet
But we will get our wellies.
Leaves falling all around,
Turning yellow on the ground.
Every garden is covered thick,
With lots of leaves in need to pick.

Imogen Nolan (7)
Corpus Christi Catholic Primary School

Loneliness

Loneliness is deep, deep black.
It tastes of mouldy cream.
Loneliness smells like rotten eggs.
It looks like an empty playground
Loneliness sounds like people having fun, except me
I hate the feel of loneliness.

Mac Reilly (7)
Corpus Christi Catholic Primary School

Hot Chocolate

Hot chocolate's lovely, warm and thick,
It slips down my throat and does the trick.
With clouds of marshmallows on the top,
I feel like I'm in heaven as I lap it up.
It takes just a spoonful of cream
To complete my dream!

Sofia Rosales-King (7)
Corpus Christi Catholic Primary School

Happiness Is Fun!

Happiness is bright yellow.
The taste of wobbly jelly.
Happiness is the smell of a chocolate waterfall
And one huge milkshake.
It sounds like laughter and joy
Happiness makes me jump!

Gyu Min Oh (7)
Corpus Christi Catholic Primary School

My Imaginary Puppy

Puppies are cute and love to play
And they're warm and cuddly every single day,
If I had a puppy I would call her Tess
But I would have to train her not to mess
I wonder how big she would be
But she would always be a best friend to me.

Mary Henry (7)
Corpus Christi Catholic Primary School

The Taste Of Excitement

Excitement is pink and purple, and tastes of strawberry ice cream,
It smells like freshly baked apple pie,
It looks like the sun shining down from the sky.
Excitement sounds like people laughing in the park on a summer's day,
And feels like someone tickling me all over until I can't breathe!

Ellemay Maher (8)
Corpus Christi Catholic Primary School

Sadness

Sadness looks like the grey cement
Its colour is dull and grey
It smells of the petrol of a car
It tastes of porridge that is rotten.

Louis Costello (8)
Corpus Christi Catholic Primary School

If

(inspired by 'If I Had Wings' by Pie Corbett)

If I had wings . . .
I would take a nap in the sky
And spread my wings like a bird.

If I had wings . . .
I would be a super hero
And save people from fire.

If I had fins . . .
I would glide through the snowy cold water
And go skiing.

If I had magic powers . . .
I would help the police
With my super strength.

Billy Smith (8)
Green Wrythe Primary School

The Animal Poems

Bethany the beautiful butterfly likes to eat loads of butter
And sleep on flowers.

Stacey the snail likes to go slow
Like a slug and make a shiny trail.

Emma the elephant has a great big trunk
And it's dark grey.

The magnificent monkey was doing a fantastic show
To all the other animals.

The crazy cat fell asleep on the bumpy road.

The gigantic gorilla was reading the newspaper.

Lauren Neck (9)
Green Wrythe Primary School

If

(inspired by 'If I Had Wings' by Pie Corbett)

If I had wings . . .
I would swoop through the clouds
And play with the birds.

If I had fins . . .
I would go through the ocean
And tease the sharks

If I had magic powers . . .
I would help people carry their bags
And help them tidy their homes.

Paige Braybrook (8)
Green Wrythe Primary School

If

(inspired by 'If I Had Wings' by Pie Corbett)

If I had wings . . .
I would glide across the clouds
And dive with the birds.

If I had fins . . .
I would swim through the foggy water
And go to New York.

If I had magic powers . . .
I would save the world
And destroy evil.

Barrie Plaistow (8)
Green Wrythe Primary School

If

(inspired by 'If I Had Wings' by Pie Corbett)

If I had wings . . .
I would fly to a shop
And grab some rainbow sweets.

If I had fins . . .
I would swim in the aquarium
And I would swim with the other fish.

If I had magic powers . . .
I would make food appear in my hands,
And eat until I was full up!

Reanna Bongo (8)
Green Wrythe Primary School

Animal Poem

Dopey dog danced all day,
Rocking rabbit was rocking,
Lippy Lion lied to me,
Cold, cold, the wind is cold as ice.

Gappy gorilla gave a speech,
Mouse Matt likes some cheese,
The tree is dark as a rainy day and as dark as the clouds.

Bethany Pickett
Green Wrythe Primary School

Untitled

The dopey dog dug up a bone in the garden
With a clever cat thinking he was cool
Sleeping in his bed.

The moaning monkey was smacking his chest
With a spider spreading himself on the glass.

Jordan Bridge (9)
Green Wrythe Primary School

If

(inspired by 'If I Had Wings' by Pie Corbett)

If I had wings . . .
I would glide across the galaxy
And fight crime

If I had wings . . .
I would swoop to China
And kill any evil.

Austin Dunnell (8)
Green Wrythe Primary School

Pets

A monkey is funny, good and very clever
He can tell jokes and bring keys to me.

The ginger cat sits and purrs all day
Drinks until he gets a belly ache.

The brown dog likes to chase balls
And bark when he sits on the park wall.

Lauren Heath (8)
Green Wrythe Primary School

Animal Crazy!

Stacey snake, sliding around on the ground.
Croaky the crocodile, croaking up in the lake
Getting a bad throat

Strikey the spider, striking cobwebs catching flies.
Monkey Mike eating bananas going mad!

Madison Dobbs (8)
Green Wrythe Primary School

The Magic Of Nature

I go to the school garden,
To eat my lunch, you see,
I'm all on my own,
Megan no-mates.

But as I sit down,
I look around,
And what do you think I see?
Magic things so beautiful,
Only I can describe them.

I see young baby birds,
Housed in trees so tall,
Branches wrapped round them,
Keeping them safe,
As I sit here all alone.

Other trees bear fruit,
So tasty and so good.
I'd love to eat it,
If I could,
As I sit here, all alone.

I'm sure I can see fairies,
Flutter their tiny wings,
Gliding up and down and round,
As I sit here, all alone.

But as I pack up to go in,
I suddenly realise,
That I am not alone at all,
But surrounded by friends,
And they are all part of
Nature.

Megan Smart (9)
Holly Lodge Primary School

Ten Pink Martians

(Inspired by 'Ten Naughty Schoolboys' by A A Milne)

Ten pink Martians,
Jumping on a line,
One fell over,
Then there were nine,

Nine pink Martians,
They were holding weights,
One couldn't hold it,
Then there were eight,

Eight pink Martians,
One turned eleven,
It was called Keven,
Then there was seven,

Seven pink Martians,
They saw a witch,
One cast away,
Then there was six,

Six pink Martians,
They were doing dives,
One went away,
Then there was five,

Five pink Martians,
They went through a door
One got caught,
Then there were four,

Four pink Martians,
One had a wee,
They all went to see,
Now there's three,

Three pink Martians,
They decided who,
But he lost his shoe,
And then there was two,

Two pink Martians,
One went in a pond,
The other came on,
Now there's one,

One pink Martian,
Tried to be a hero,
It was a weirdo,
Now there's zero.

Hannah Southerton (11)
Holly Lodge Primary School

Animals In The Jungle

In the jungle there are many animals
Here are some.

Marvellous, messy monkeys
Swing from tree to tree
In the canopy.

Tragic, tiny tigers
Creeping on the forest floor.

Shiny, shaking snakes
Slithering from branch to branch
In the understory.

Lively lions
Walking slowly on the forest floor.

Twittering toucans
Flying in the sky.

Slow sloths
Climbing down a tree
At a slow speed.

But now it's being destroyed
So help us change this.
So it is a silent place again.

Lucy Verrinder (8)
Holly Lodge Primary School

Ten Little Aliens

(inspired by 'Ten Naughty Schoolboys' by A A Milne)

Ten little aliens
Marching in a line
One fell over
And then there were nine.

Nine little aliens
Looking at a gate
One looked and fell
And then there were eight.

Eight little aliens
Looking into heaven
One broke his arm
And then there were seven.

Seven little aliens
Showing off with sticks
One fainted on the ground
And then there were six.

Six little aliens
Playing with a beehive
One got stung
And then there were five.

Five little aliens
Knocking on a door
One ran away
And then there were four.

Four little aliens
Climbing up a tree
One fell down
And then there were three.

Three little aliens
Playing shout boo
One got scared
And then there were two.

Two little aliens
Playing in the sun
One got burnt
And then there was one.

One little alien
Having lots of fun
He got bored
And then there were none!

Megan Rafano (10)
Holly Lodge Primary School

Diggers

Dig, dig, dig
Dig all day
Dig, dig, dig
From day to day

Dig, dig, dig
Dig round and round
Dig, dig, dig
Scrape up the ground

Dig, dig, dig
Digging all day
Dig, dig, digging
From near to faraway

Dig, dig, digging
Digging like we say
Dig, dig, digging
The happy way

Dig, dig, dig
We've dug all day
Dig, dig, dig
Every way!

Jessica Gardner (9)
Holly Lodge Primary School

Little Aliens

(inspired by 'Ten Naughty Schoolboys' by A A Milne)

Ten little aliens,
Sitting quite fine,
One slid off,
Then there were nine.

Nine little aliens,
Saying 'Hi mate',
He walked off,
Then there were eight.

Eight little aliens,
Walking up to heaven,
One fell down,
Then there were seven.

Seven little aliens,
Picking up sticks,
One didn't join in,
Then there were six.

Six little aliens,
Standing alive,
One dropped dead,
Then there were five.

Five little aliens,
Busy with a chore,
One didn't want to,
Then there were four.

Four little aliens,
Climbing a tree,
Blob was afraid of heights,
Then there were three.

Three little aliens,
Shouting out boo,
One went deaf,
Then there were two.

Two little aliens,
Being so dumb,
Blab tried to be clever,
Then there was one.

One little alien,
Having lots of fun,
He got bored,
Then there was none!

Ellie Edwards (11)
Holly Lodge Primary School

Uranus

Uranus.
Huge and cold,
Blue and green,
Surrounded by,
Black rings.

Uranus.
Icy moons,
All around,
Never making,
The slightest sound.

Uranus.
Oddly spins,
So night in parts,
For forty years,
Can sometimes last.

Uranus.
Largest of the planet's moons,
Titania, Shakespeare's Fairy Queen,
In a 'Midsummer Night's Dream',
Lets off an enormous gleam.

Priya Manda (10)
Holly Lodge Primary School

Ten Big Rockets

(inspired by 'Ten Naughty Schoolboys' by A A Milne)

Ten big rockets
Flying in a line,
One flew off,
Then there were nine.

Nine big rockets
Playing with their mates,
One lost his ball,
Then there were eight.

Eight big rockets
Waiting to go to heaven,
One passed away,
Then there were seven.

Seven big rockets
Trying hard to mix,
One forgot his name
Then there were six.

Six big rockets
Trying to survive,
One hit a planet,
Then there were five.

Five big rockets
Learning to open a door,
One exploded,
Then there were four.

Four big rockets
Climbing up a tree,
One lost his balance,
Then there were three.

Three big rockets
Trying to tie a shoe,
One fell over,
Then there was two.

Two big rockets
Visited their mum,
One got told off,
Then there was one.

One big rocket
Wanted to be a hero,
One jumped off a building,
Then there was zero.

Amy Whittam (11)
Holly Lodge Primary School

Big Bully Bulldozer Destroys Our School

The big bully bulldozer is a grumpy beast,
Working by him is Baby Bulldozer,
Grumpy Green Machine
And
Revolting Red Robot.

Grumpy Green Machine, flattens our land,
With heavy wheels he destroys our sandpits
And now we have nowhere to play,
He grumbles and groans and moans,
On top of his head are flashing lights,
Powerful enough to blind you!

Big Bully Bulldozer digs his teeth into the ground,
With teeth like lions he eats his way through our school field,
Revolting Red Robot help his companion Baby
Bulldozer chomp away our adventure trail
And all our favourite toys,
They scream and roar, whistle and climb
Slowly up the mountains of doom!

Hazel Fanning (9)
Holly Lodge Primary School

Ten Tiny Comets

(Inspired by 'Ten Naughty Schoolboys' by A A Milne)

Ten little comets
Flying in a line,
One blew up,
Then there were nine.

Nine tiny comets
Trying to find mates,
One got lost,
Then there were eight.

Eight tiny comets
Looking up to heaven,
One stopped burning,
Then there were seven.

Seven tiny comets
Needing to be fired,
One jumped into a taxi,
Then there were six.

Six tiny comets
All so alive,
One ran off,
Then there were five.

Five tiny comets
Having their tea,
One got a bus,
Then there were three.

Three tiny comets,
All shouting 'Boo!'
One tripped over
Then there were two.

Two tiny comets
Having lots of fun,
One deflated,
Then there was one.

One tiny comet
Staring at the sun,
he got too close
Then there were none.

James Howell (10)
Holly Lodge Primary School

Jungle

The cheetahs jog
While lions sleep
Like a log.

The snakes lurk
While frogs are jerked
By the rain.

Up above
The lion pants
While the march of the ants is down below.

5 turtles swim down
10 turtles have a race
They all hurtle to the line.

Just as the sun begins
A storm of dust
From the logger's machines!

Flight of the bird
The battle begins
Man and animal fight for land.

Samuel Casey (8)
Holly Lodge Primary School

What Can I See From The Playground?

Is there anything to see?
Brown dust is blinding me.
The great JCB,
Is deafening me.
It's gobbled up the sandpit,
And swallowed the field whole.
The bulldozers roar,
It's impossible to ignore.
Try to get to sleep,
As my best friend starts to weep.
The red TD trugs along,
As it clears away an exploded bomb.
There's a giant mountain of mud,
That falls down with a thud.
It leaves behind a giant track,
As it steadily drives back.
The next thing you know it's coming your way,
Which gives a perfect end to the day.

Rachel Ferguson (10)
Holly Lodge Primary School

The Giant Bully Bulldozer

Outside our classroom window,
The giant fighting bully
Has swallowed up our field,
Frantically digging holes
Tears down our classrooms.

Outside our classroom window
A volcano of mud,
Towers over our head
Trying to concentrate is hopeless,
It is impossible to ignore.

Anna Burton (9)
Holly Lodge Primary School

The Rainforest

Enter a rainforest of green
Leaves everywhere making umbrellas
With huge trees anywhere you look

Cute and cuddly monkeys
As black as wet soil
Sitting on a thin branch
Playing and being friends together

Turtles with speckles of colours
Swimming through the water with piranhas
Being friends together
Having fun too

Now enter an unhappy jungle
No green anywhere
Cut-down, dry old trees
Animals in panic trying to save each other
How did it happen?
Why?

Joshua Elsey (8)
Holly Lodge Primary School

The Deep, Dark Rainforest

The dark brown cuddly bear walked through the swishy, damp green leaves,
Though the rainforest.

The cute little monkeys are swinging from branch to branch
While their mummies and daddies are hunting for their food.

The sneaky snakes are slithering up the tree to hunt!

The golden jaguar walks through the rainforest
To hunt for its prey!

The loving lizard drops off a tree to the ground
And slowly changes from brown to a light green!

Nadia R Elghor (8)
Holly Lodge Primary School

The Magic Box

(Inspired by 'Magic Box' by Kit Wright)

I will put in the box . . .
The smell of a delicious roast dinner,
The clip-clop of horses trotting along the path,
The golden and red leaves falling off the trees.

I will put in the box . . .
The cry of a newborn baby,
The lovely taste of a rare fish,
And the first cuddly teddy bear.

I will put in the box . . .
The most colourful rainbow ever in the countryside,
The golden sand from Africa's desert,
And the first ever penny farthing bike.

I will put in the box . . .
The most beautiful pink petals on a flower,
The first pound in my pocket,
And the taste of lovely chocolate.

Laura Hutchinson (8)
Holly Lodge Primary School

The Roaring Bulldozer

The roaring bulldozers are noisily working outside,
Inside children are staring like French fries,
Suddenly, the big demolishers storm into the school grounds,
Pouncing like little hounds,
As their big, yellow partner tells them to go,
They fell into the classroom where everyone stares,
What are you doing?
Everyone stares,
Then they remember their work.
So the big, yellow beast climbs back up the castle of mud.
Just like a wasp whizzes,
It's just like boom, bomb bop!

Emma Verrinder (9)
Holly Lodge Primary School

The Magic Box

(Inspired by 'Magic Box' by Kit Wright)

I will put in the box . . .
The delightful dolphins dancing in the deep blue sea,
The sound of crabs scuttling along the soft sand,
The owls hooting in the treetops.

I will put in the box . . .
The softness from a small, fluffy rabbit,
The tiny seed from a super sunflower,
The sizzling of a sausage in a pan.

I will put in the box . . .
The sparkle of a star by the sea,
The delicious taste of chocolate fudge cake,
The tweeting of baby bluebirds in their neat nest.

I will put in the box . . .
The kindness of a mum called Katie,
The marvellous taste of delicious marshmallows,
The swish of the tops of trees on a windy day.

Kiera Nixon (7)
Holly Lodge Primary School

Jungle Animals

Welcome to the jungle,
You will see lots of animals.

The snakes slither over the branches,
The lions sleep in their dens,
The monkeys swing to different branches.

The parrots repeat you,
The toucans are squawking and pecking,
The jaguar is leaping for its prey,
The monkeys jump around quickly,
The frogs are hopping around on lily pads,
The crocodile is hiding in the water.

Lewis Wood (8)
Holly Lodge Primary School

The Magic Box

(Inspired by 'Magic Box' by Kit Wright)

I will put in the box . . .
A pretty, pale rainbow sitting in a field,
The seagull's squawk on the seaside,
The smell of the liquid my mummy uses for ironing.

I will put in the box . . .
The fluffy, big bear I have up in my bedroom,
The soothing taste of brown, black or white chocolate,
The crash of lightning's strike.

I will put in the box . . .
The crash and the bang of fireworks exploding,
The wonderful smell of omelette,
The sweet taste of lollies.

I will put in the box . . .
The soft, silky fur that gerbils have,
The salty McDonald's chips,
The cute faces that my silly sister has.

Lauren Winter (7)
Holly Lodge Primary School

Beauty Or A Dump?

Monkeys in the trees terrified of the noise,
Tigers pouncing, jaguars running to safety.
The lion cubs trying their best
To escape from the falling trees.
The jade-green leaves scatter everywhere.

A man scaring off the animals for a dare.
For two weeks more and more bulldozers,
Come and destroy the rainforest.
Two months have passed
And all the bulldozers are gone
And the rainforest is no more.

Eden Robinson (8)
Holly Lodge Primary School

The Chopped Down Rainforest

Animals get cross
And try to stop
The towering logs
Getting chopped down.
Like a meteor hitting earth
Or a bomb hitting the rainforest
Animals fly, swig or walk away
Thinking of the lovely, beautiful place
With lots of green things, with infinite trees!
But now when they look
It is like an old, dark brown treeless graveyard!
Families get killed by big bulging bulldozers crushing their skin.
Like a giant foot.
All the old, bold trees
Get conquered and
Smashed!
And then animals take one last look and. . .
Go . . .

Charlie Carr (9)
Holly Lodge Primary School

Shiny, Yellow Digger

Giant scoop like a robot,
Demolishing a classroom,
Leaving just a colossal footprint,
Zigzagged treads,
Imprinting lines in the dirt,
Castle of mud with Mum on the top,
Family of bulldozers; Mum yellow, Dad a truck,
Little boy is red and little girl is white,
Mountain of mud like a volcano,
The other day I thought I saw,
Bob the Builder at the door!

Phillippa Collins (9)
Holly Lodge Primary School

The Magic Box

(Inspired by 'Magic Box' by Kit Wright)

I will put in the box . . .
A boy who is playing in the long street.
I will put in the box . . .
A roast dinner with some roses in the back.
The hot hands from my hot chocolate.
I will put in the box . . .
A big, black dog with a skinny, swishing tail.
I will put in the box . . .
A big, popping firework that will fly in the sky,
The smashing football going in the goal,
The sun popping in the shining blue sky.
I will put in the box . . .
The sparkling, silver robot.
I will put in the box . . .
A fox trying to get a bird.
I will put in the box . . .
A big wolf swimming in the ice-cold water.

Hayden Bowen (7)
Holly Lodge Primary School

The Dead Rainforest

The bulldozers and machines
Getting ready to attack the rainforest.

The poor trees lying on the ground
The angry cheetah growling at his home.

The sound of the trees
Are smashing on the wet surface
Like a volcano erupting
With a bomb.

The big machines tearing the trees in half
And crushing the ground
Like an angry, giant's footstep.

Hasan Iqbal (8)
Holly Lodge Primary School

Bullying Bulldozers

B uddies, one small, one big.
U ndergoing the procedure, with no care in the world.
L ike father, like son.
L onging for them to go because I'm trying to concentrate.
Y ou wouldn't want to be in their way.

B uilding up a volcanic mountain of mud.
U sing different diggers everyday annoys me so much.
L azily the king climbs up the castle whilst the servant digs.
L ooking at them is making me sick.
D igging up mud, trying to make it flat but instead it's lumpy.
O ver they go waddling from side to side.
Z onks of weeks they've been here and all they've done is dig.
E veryone's waiting for them to finish.
R oaring as they roll along.
S eriously they ate our sandpit, they ate our field and worst of all
they ate our new hockey puck!
Bang!

Samantha Best (9)
Holly Lodge Primary School

The Jungle

In the jungle where the monkeys sleep.
It is quiet as the evening peeps.

Trees are green
Tree trunks are red
Soon everything in the jungle shall be dead.

Men with machines
Cutting down trees
More and more pollution for the bees.

Less and less trees
Less and less fleas
Deserts turning into seas.

George Lowery (8)
Holly Lodge Primary School

The Bully Bulldozer

As we stare absent-mindedly out of the window,
All we see is mud and bulldozers.
But it will finally show,
When we get our new classroom.

The mean machine ate up our hockey puck,
And gulped our sandpit (hooray!)
One day a machine arrived, and with luck,
We got to see it working.

It started roaring
And clanking
Doing its robot thing
Dancing madly all day.

It nearly bashed up our classroom,
We thought It would have us for lunch,
We nearly had to close the blinds,
And then it went crunch!

Emily Briggs (9)
Holly Lodge Primary School

Mustangs

M ay we be free from those horrible men.
U s horses are mustangs, we must be free.
S tand proud to be horses.
T ell history that we will be free until Man stops us.
A nd life makes us mainly heard, but never caught with powerful tyres.
N ow we're learning to live as one, horses and humans must become one.
G ang against the humans who cares now? All we want to be is free.
Mustangs must be. . .free!

Ellie Doudican (10)
Holly Lodge Primary School

Worst Of The Jungle

The wild wind,
Blows,
The clouds come,
And go,
Something's coming,
Loud and furious,
Cutting and chopping,
Painfully,
Scaring and creeping,
Animals away.

The birds staring,
At their,
Ruined homes,
A symbol of death,
And,
Sadness.

Lottie Head (8)
Holly Lodge Primary School

The Magic Box

(Inspired by 'Magic Box' by Kit Wright)

I will put in the box . . .
Six sizzling sausages sitting on the barbecue,
A beautiful little butterfly fluttering in the air,
Ten fat burgers cooking in the oven.

I will put in the box . . .
Two fat, red lions,
Twenty big, grey bears sitting on the floor,
Seven small frogs sitting on a lily pad.

I will put in the box . . .
A horse riding me to the farm,
The bright sun shining in my eyes,
Some jelly beans from the shops.

Matthew Hunt (7)
Holly Lodge Primary School

The Destruction Of The Rainforest

Monkeys swing tree to tree
If the trees aren't there then the monkeys can't swing tree to tree
What will they eat?

It will look like a mess like we make in our bedrooms
It will be horror to animals!
It was heaven, now it's hell
It's a symbol of death!
Jaguars, cheetahs and panthers growling ferociously at the people being unkind.
It will be a dull, torn place with animals homeless!
Destroyed, a cheetah crawls looking at its prey
The floor rumbles, animals look at the people who are cutting the trees down,
Saying bye-bye to their homes
Monkeys looking at the people nervously, watching what the people are doing.

Harrison Button (8)
Holly Lodge Primary School

The Magic Box

(Inspired by 'Magic Box' by Kit Wright)

I will put in the box . . .
The smoky smell of sizzling potatoes,
The lovely hot, melting chocolate,
The beautiful colour of beetroot.

I will put in the box . . .
A kind sight of flowers in the garden,
An elegant, black horse trotting in the field,
A grey elephant walking with a big herd.

I will put in the box . . .
A little goldfish giggling in the water,
A big boy talking to his friends,
A cute little bunny rabbit hopping in a cage.

Rebecca Hoare (7)
Holly Lodge Primary School

Untitled

Crocodiles in the river
Snapping their huge jaws

Parrots flying through the trees
Repeating what you say
Annoying the other animals
Whilst sitting in a tree

Lions sleeping in their den
Snoozing lazily

Monkeys swinging in the trees
Eating any bananas they find

Elephants trampling down the trees
Laughing at the monkeys' tricks

Frogs jumping, catching flies
As well as swimming in the pools.

Lucy Green (8)
Holly Lodge Primary School

The Big Mud Monster

B old
I gnoring
G iant

M onstrous
U gly
D irty

M uddy
O utbreak
N aughty
S trong
T earing
E ating
R egret.

Rebecca Eastwell (9)
Holly Lodge Primary School

The Crushers

Dancing in the blazing sun,
They stop at night,
It's morning,
They do the robot,
Once again!

I think we were wrong
To let them destroy our classrooms,
Oh no!
A man's coming in the scary machine,
Run!

I can hear a noise
It sounds like a gun,
Oh no! *Bang!*
It's the bulldozing bully.
Run!

Matthew Hyde (9)
Holly Lodge Primary School

Dangerous

Monkeys on the great Rapor tree swinging, jumping and playing free.

Monkeys with no home
Scared, underground and happy no more.

The tigers like Shere Khan, waiting for their prey at the end of the day.

The tigers that are not like Shere Khan, beastly quick and never waiting,
They'll be dead in seconds!

There are a lot more animals than what I am saying
But most are dangerous!
Like coyotes , piranhas. Cheetahs and pythons
They are all dangerous!

Harvey Brewer Allan (8)
Holly Lodge Primary School

Planet Mercury

Mercury.
Scorching and huge,
Orange and red,
Boiling hot,
Messenger of the gods.

Mercury.
Hot by day,
Cold by night
Doesn't contain life.

Mercury.
Orbit in 88 days
Hotter than Earth
Cold and heavy.

Mercury.

Morgan Coward (11)
Holly Lodge Primary School

The Edge Of Extinction

The rainforest
Strong and powerful,
Home to all animals.
Big and small.
Need a home.
From the buzzing bumble bee
To the tiny ant!

The bulldozers come and crush the rainforest.
Scattering trees from side to side.
Cheetahs, monkeys, jaguars and birds.
Flee.
Never to see their homes again.
The ruined rainforest.
A symbol of death.

Morgan Decanter-Morris (8)
Holly Lodge Primary School

No More Rainforest

Where once was paradise, life and peace.
Now lies death.
All that's visible is dead
Wrecked trees
Nothing lives here
All the lives lost
As the monstrous machines crush
Everything in their path
As every animal that's lost its home watches
They are outraged
In fury
But don't dare to try to stop them
Crash! Goes another tree as it is knocked down
All this is known as a symbol of
Disaster and death.

James Upfield (8)
Holly Lodge Primary School

What Happens To The Jungle

Shady brown branches
Emerald-green leaves,
Tweeting birds,
Graceful monkeys,
Gentle rustlings, high and low
In the beautiful jungle.

Animals die slowly in distress,
Homes are being cut down,
Trucks come to take the logs,
It's all happening fast.

Now
Dead silence floats through the
Destroyed jungle
Dead logs and sticks lie in a dull graveyard.

Emma Wakley (8)
Holly Lodge Primary School

The Bully, Burglar, Baddie Bulldozer

There's a destroyer of our sandpit,
Plus our climbing frame too,
It's like Bob the Builder's at our school,
Why doesn't it pick on someone its own size too?

JCB makes a noise that's impossible to ignore,
Bang goes the bulldozer,
Crash goes the crane,
See, impossible to ignore.

The JCB's on a mound of mud,
A castle of mud on the field,
The next thing you know it's climbing away,
Might it fall one day?

Emma Nash (9)
Holly Lodge Primary School

Animals In The Jungle

Jaguars running
People cutting down trees
Animals howling
Buzzing bees in the trees

Pandas eating bamboo
Koalas swinging in the trees in the sun
Whilst eating eucalyptus trees

Monkeys swinging through the trees
Scorpions below
Elephants laughing at the monkeys' tricks

Piranhas showing off their teeth
Stingrays stinging
Crocodiles snapping their jaws.

Chelsea Morhall (8)
Holly Lodge Primary School

What's Happening To The Rainforest?

The black monkeys sit in branchy trees.
The monkeys' cry is filling the jungle.

It's almost always raining in the jungle.
When the monkeys jump
Water sprinkles off the leaves.

Suddenly big *bulldozers* come.
Men start cutting down the trees.
Animals get hurt.

Then a road is built.
Trees are being picked up and being taken away.

Animals have to go to different parts of the rainforest to live.

Paige Dann (8)
Holly Lodge Primary School

The Magic Box

(Inspired by 'Magic Box' by Kit Wright)

I will put in the box . . .
Crazy Connie reading her silly book,
Swaying trees moving in the night breeze,
The wonderful taste of a bit of chocolate in hot chocolate.

I will put in the box . . .
The pretty rocks that get wet every day,
The smoky smell of chips when they are on the BBQ,
The sweet music of cool bands.

I will put in the box . . .
The nice smell of the breeze in the air.
The people playing happily,
The green apple so tasty to everyone.

Sophie Carr (7)
Holly Lodge Primary School

Rainforest Gone

Two little cheeky, furry, black monkeys
Sitting quietly
On a light brown branch.
The smallest monkey,
Staring wildly at the luminous green leaves
With its big, bold eyes

Suddenly
The rainforest is being cut down
The trees are in pain
While the ants climb over them
On the dusty ground
A wiggling worm can't find its way
As it climbs over the trees.

Sasha Luff (8)
Holly Lodge Primary School

The Big, Yellow Wasp

It stings the ground,
Like a wasp stinging an innocent person,
Making a horrible sound,

The builders drink their cups of tea,
Having their break,
Scratching away their fleas,

It breaks my toys,
I don't have anything left to play with
I wonder if it could eat the boys?

I couldn't eat my tea,
I couldn't believe it,
Why did it have to happen to me?

Laura Wills (10)
Holly Lodge Primary School

The Magic Box
(Inspired by 'Magic Box' by Kit Wright)

I will put in the box . . .
A big firework
And an exploding rocket zooming through the sky.

I will put in the box . . .
A toy car that I can race
And it is fast.

I will put in the box . . .
A friendly grey rabbit
With a fluffy, soft tail.

I will put in the box . . .
A big monster that sucks people's blood.

Charlie Lucy (7)
Holly Lodge Primary School

Macbeth

Macbeth, Macbeth, bravest of all.
Macbeth, Macbeth, strong and tall.
Macbeth, Macbeth, Thane of Glamis.
Macbeth, Macbeth, bravest of all.

Macbeth, Macbeth, met the witches.
Macbeth, Macbeth, alongside Banquo.
Macbeth, Macbeth, scared out of his kilt.

The witches greeted Macbeth weirdly
Macbeth, Macbeth, was confused,
Something strange upon the heath,
Macbeth was stroking his beard as
The three witches disappeared.

George Lucy (9)
Holly Lodge Primary School

Ruined Rainforest

Big bulging tree trunks as big as cranes.
Insects buzz around the jungle.
The birds fly up with the butterflies,
A crocodile lying peacefully on the water.
Monkeys chatting continuously,
Picking bugs out of each others hair.

Once was a lush green jungle teeming with life.
But now only a brown, dull graveyard of dead trees.

Slowly the bulldozers crush the rainforest,
Rainforest conquered by the bulldozers.
The rainforest looks like a meteor has hit it.
There are no animals living there anymore.

Samuel Hymas (9)
Holly Lodge Primary School

The Culprit Of The Ruins

The culprit of the old school ruins,
Is lurking in the dirt,
Under a mud mountain that's about to erupt like a volcano,
It's swallowing the dirt from underneath like a tiger attacking its prey,
Mysterious patterns begin to emerge ending at the foot of the ever-exploding volcano . . .

The crater is getting deeper and deeper like a dried up river,
It is impossible to ignore as it paws at the ground with claws as sharp as knives,
It moves like a robot tipping lava at the ever-growing volcano.

It gets louder and louder as it bangs at the ground again and again demolishing our school field.

Georgia Herrington (10)
Holly Lodge Primary School

There, Then Gone

The playful monkeys,
Are in the splendid
Rainforest
Then,

Suddenly. . .
The bulldozers come
Crash!

The rainforests is gone
Now there's nothing
Nothing at all.

Amy Stevens (9)
Holly Lodge Primary School

Beauty To Destruction

Welcome to the rainforest,
The beauty of the world,
Where tigers run and insects scatter.

But no longer does that remain,
The insects are crushed,
The tigers have fled, we have now said bye-bye to the trees.
This forest you see is now a symbol of death to you and me.

The animals are back with lots
Of hope but sadly
The trees are still broken.

Jack Reid (8)
Holly Lodge Primary School

Destruction Of The Rainforest

The deserted rainforest,
Has slowly lost all its habitats
And so it becomes,
More like a desert.

The animals flee
From this sad devastation.
And they'll
Never be parents again.

We do not raise this,
But the rainforest is quickly getting destroyed.

Joseph Neal (8)
Holly Lodge Primary School

Deforestation

As the hot sun beats down like a meteor,
The sweaty men get their axes ready,
They get in their huge bulldozers,
Get them ready to destroy.

The dead, dull brown branches just lie there,
Like they're asleep
The crushed dirty leaves just lie there.

As the men come the rivers get bigger and bigger.
Even taller than me.
A great storm comes like thunder as the men walk away.

Cameron Watson (9)
Holly Lodge Primary School

My Poetry Box

(Inspired by 'Magic Box' by Kit Wright)

The things I'll put in my poetry box are . . .

A really big poetry book full of funny poems,
A tiny blue raindrop that's fallen from the fluffy, white clouds
And a big chunk of the peppery, hot sun in the bright yellow colour.

My box is very pretty and delicate,
Made from silver, gold, wood and jewels,
With diamonds on the outside
And inside it has lots of lovely butterflies.
The butterflies peek out when you open it.

Ellie Heritage (7)
Holly Lodge Primary School

My Super Secret Box

(Inspired by 'Magic Box' by Kit Wright)

I will put in my super secret box . . .

Some shiny, silver bullets which were found down the road,
Some super secret wishes written down in code
And the lawnmower racing round the garden.

My box is classic
And made from gold, silver and bronze
With jewels on the outside.
In it there are cobwebs.
It also glows in the dark.

Thomas Ferguson (8)
Holly Lodge Primary School

My Special Box

(Inspired by 'Magic Box' by Kit Wright)

In my special box I will put . . .
The light of the bright sun shining in the sky,
The hop of a rabbit under the muddy ground
And the sparkle of an eel under the blue sea.

My box is old and rusty
And made from pure bronze and silver
With a wooden drawbridge outside.
In the middle of the box there is a slim dinosaur
With spikes on his back.

Ethan Court (7)
Holly Lodge Primary School

My Poetry Box

(Inspired by 'Magic Box' by Kit Wright)

In my box I will put . . .

The spark of the stars in the dark night sky,
The colours of the rainbow which shine in the sun
And the drop of the rain falling from the sky.

My box is sparkly and made from shiny jewels,
With multicoloured spots on the outside
And tiny little fairies hidden in the corners.
When you open it, stars fly out.

Emily Couper (7)
Holly Lodge Primary School

Venus

Deadly acid fills the air,
Massive volcanoes everywhere,
Higher than any mountain on earth,
That is Venus right from birth.

Emily Stillwell (10)
Holly Lodge Primary School

My Lost And Found Box

(Inspired by 'Magic Box' by Kit Wright)

In my lost and found box there is . . .

A dazzling star from the dark night sky,
A sweet candy cane from a beautiful sweet factory
And the blue waves from the sea swishing to shore.

My box is sparkly and made out of sterling silver
With shiny stars and delicate gems on the outside
And fairy wishes in the corners.
It has colourful butterflies lightly fluttering out of the box.

Rosie Boddy (7)
Holly Lodge Primary School

The Lush, Green Rainforest

Massive shady branches rustle in the shimmering light.
Black, furry monkeys chatter in the treetop branches.
Shiny, tasty mango fruit hangs among the lush, green leaves
Where the fresh wind blows.

Deep, damp floor.
Grey mist floating in the air where the dead
Dull, brown trees have been destroyed
Animals lying on the deep, damp floor
Have nowhere to live anymore.

Chloe Rees (8)
Holly Lodge Primary School

Diggers

A shiny, yellow digger
Grinding up the mud.
Scooping like a spoon
Crushing the brown, orange and gold mud.
Dust flicking after every scoop.

Jamie Weston (9)
Holly Lodge Primary School

Beauty Or A Dump?

In the rainforest where all loving animals live
The panthers roar to make the jungle wake.
Bulldozers hit the trees like a meteor from outer space,
Making a beautiful rainforest like a graveyard of burnt destroyed trees.

All the animals have a last look
When they blink its like a zap of lightning
All the rainforest has been destroyed.
A brown, dry, deserted wasteland.

Peter Sivill (8)
Holly Lodge Primary School

The Lonely Fish

There once was a lonely fish,
His name was Franky Bean,
He longed for a friend for years and years,
But nobody was too keen!

Then one day an alien arrived,
They stood together side by side,
Then they got married,
The alien was carried
And they both lived together for their really long life.

Liberty Balmer (11)
Holly Lodge Primary School

The School Crushers

The rough, big yellow beast climbs slowly up the volcano mountain
Terrorising our school.
All the teachers running away because the school won't last a day.

Digging up the school's ground
Making lots of holes jumping up and down on the moles' holes.

Kieran Burr (9)
Holly Lodge Primary School

The Magic Box
(Inspired by 'Magic Box' by Kit Wright)

I will put in the box . . .
The fiery fireworks high up in the sky,
The sizzling sausages in a saucepan,
A beautiful butterfly soaring through the sky.

I will put in the box . . .
The tooting of a terrific trumpet,
The golden sight of the sun over the desert,
The smoothest and softest stone in the world.

Joshua Thorne (7)
Holly Lodge Primary School

The Magic Box
(Inspired by 'Magic Box' by Kit Wright)

I will put in the box . . .
A pretty silk dress from India,
The clipping of crabs pinching their claws,
The sweet smell of lovely pizza.

I will put in the box . . .
A playful puppy that is a Labrador,
The funny faces my annoying sister has,
A line of smelly stickers.

Rachel Evans (8)
Holly Lodge Primary School

My Scary Box
(Inspired by 'Magic Box' by Kit Wright)

My box is ancient
And made from ice and snow
With dinosaur bones on the lid
Its hinges are rusty
Because it is old.

James Tyler Batchelor (7)
Holly Lodge Primary School

The Magic Box
(Inspired by 'Magic Box' by Kit Wright)

I will put in the box . . .
Ten jellyfish dangling their tentacles at the turtles,
The smell of burnt bacon on the barbecue,
The teddy bear turning in the twilight.

I will put in the box . . .
The tweeting sound of singing birds in the tree,
The beautiful taste of orange cheese
And marvellous milk.

Tommy Brook (7)
Holly Lodge Primary School

My Imaginary Box
(Inspired by 'Magic Box' by Kit Wright)

In my imaginary box
I see myself in my mind travelling around the world.
Feeling all the water on my body whilst training for the Olympics,
And fighting all the evil people to protect the world.

My box is a classic box and made from marble
With hopes and dreams on the inside
And stars, glitter and leather outside.
When you open it, it sings a lovely tune.

Emily Bunch (7)
Holly Lodge Primary School

The Destroyed Rainforest

The cute black monkeys, perched quietly on a long grey branch,
Looking in disgrace at the dull destroyed rainforest.
All the insects are getting squashed.
The dusty bulldozer rushing into the jungle.
All the animals become homeless staring at their dull ruined homes.

Harry Dean (9)
Holly Lodge Primary School

My Creative Box

(Inspired by 'Magic Box' by Kit Wright)

In my box I will put . . .
A Celtic and Roman soldier going to the big battle on the hill
While Queen Boudicca charges on her cart.
A shooting star all the way from the sky in Mexico
And an ice cream that never melts, even in the hot, golden sun.

My box is starry and made from leather and pearls,
With stars and glitter and shiny paper on the outside.
Inside there are fairies and twinkles in the air.

Ella Bowdery (8)
Holly Lodge Primary School

The Magic Box

(Inspired by 'Magic Box' by Kit Wright)

I will put in the box . . .
A firework popping in the sky,
A sparkling Christmas tree in the house,
A scary shark swimming in the sea.

I will put in the box . . .
A scary vampire dripping with Hallowe'en blood,
The sweet smell of Christmas dinner,
A rattlesnake slithering across the desert.

Thomas Howell (7)
Holly Lodge Primary School

Take A Sneaky Look

If you take a look in the jungle you will find. . .
Cute, soft and furry, cuddly monkeys
Take a look at the monkeys make a shelter or a home
With the rustling leaves
And take a peep at the slithering, sticky, slimy carpet python snakes!

Amie Parry (9)
Holly Lodge Primary School

My Secret Box

(Inspired by 'Magic Box' by Kit Wright)

In my box I will put . . .
A big white shark snapping his teeth,
A smiley monkey in the tree
And a cowboy toy looking at me.

My box is new and made from gold,
With dots on the outside
And in it is hard, hard wood.
It is very expensive.

Adam Richardson (7)
Holly Lodge Primary School

The Dino Box

(Inspired by 'Magic Box' by Kit Wright)

In my box I will put . . .
A fierce triceratops and a mighty T-rex,
A spiny stegosaurus and a skinny Troodon
And a fast allosaurus chasing its prey.

My box has ice inside
And dinosaur bones outside.
It has fancy gold and silver sides.
When I open it, dinosaurs jump up.

Jay Bibey (7)
Holly Lodge Primary School

Trees In The Jungle

Lovely tree trunks are so
Tough and bumpy
The trees are so messy
And the leaves are green
The monkeys are swinging in the treetops.

Jack Banyard (8)
Holly Lodge Primary School

The Magic Box

(Inspired by 'Magic Box' by Kit Wright)

I will put in the box . . .
A scary shark sitting in the sea,
The wattling and weaving with Luica,
The sweet smell of chocolate.

I will put in the box . . .
A sweet sound of a singing choir,
The salty sea waving around and around,
The hungry lions lying on the sand.

Connie White (7)
Holly Lodge Primary School

Destroyed Rainforest

Once the rainforest was beautiful
Now it is a disgrace to nature
Once there were monkeys swinging around
Now they are scared to
Now snakes can't hang from many trees
The rainforest becomes a bundle of logs
Not many animals can live in rainforests
Now when a tree is cut down
An animal has lost its home.

Benjamin White (8)
Holly Lodge Primary School

The Digger

I'm gigantic, I'm enormous, huge shiny and brown,
I like to clank around the world from dawn till sundown,
Japan to Beijing, I have been there to make and destroy those cities all,
I have a very busy day but it is all worth it all for the sake of the day,
At night I sleep like a log as well as just dreaming of work delights.

Kathryn Evans (9)
Holly Lodge Primary School

The Jungle

Monkeys swing from tree to tree
Leaves rustling all over the tree
Snakes slithering up the tall trees
Jaguars charging at the birds
Bears roaring and menacing
Tigers tearing skin
Rapid water waving
Snapping crocodiles wait
Patiently for their prey.

William Dowdell (8)
Holly Lodge Primary School

Jungle Town

The ground is so clean
The trees are so tall
The smell really reeks
The logs are so thick
The leaves are so freaky and big
The flowers are bright
The lake is like glass
The sun is so hot
And the vines are growing so quickly.

Billy Savell (8)
Holly Lodge Primary School

Bully Bulldozer

Big Yellow Bully and Junior Red, break our stuff,
Destroy our hut.

It's a big plump monster who eats our earth.

He's got a big green friend called Mr Dragon.

Big Yellow Bully scraping the ground as he turns around.

Charlotte Parker-Joyce (9)
Holly Lodge Primary School

The Jungle

The little monkeys are swinging sweetly across the light brown branches.
Snakes are slithering sneakily to their lunch.
A golden and beautiful jaguar is strolling around the jungle for food.
Crazy caterpillars are running around very fast on the forest floor.
Explorers are getting their binoculars out
And looking for unusual creatures.
Creepy crocodiles are sneakily getting in the swamp
And are trying to scare the other animals.

Taylor McFadden (8)
Holly Lodge Primary School

Saturn

One of the most extraordinary sights,
Smooth, yellowish tinge,
Two giant bands surround it,
Closing in, in, in,
Eighteen moons it has so far,
Spins quickly around the sun,
Circled by bands of clouds,
Saturn,
Sixth from the sun.

Katie Spicer (10)
Holly Lodge Primary School

Dig, Dig

Dig, dig, that's all I want to do.
Do it here, do it there.
Dig, dig, every day I do,
Dig, dig, what I love to do,
Excuse me, I've got some working to do!

Kimberley Wilson (9)
Holly Lodge Primary School

The Bully

The big bully bulldozer twists around
And digs anything in his sight.

It's like an explosion of mud.
Clawing the ground like an eagle!
Whilst turning around it screams
Like a ghost!

I can barely hear myself think!
What should I do?

Amba Welling (9)
Holly Lodge Primary School

My Treasure Box
(Inspired by 'Magic Box' by Kit Wright)

In my treasure box I will put . . .

A cruiser in the harbour in Monte Carlo,
The big, blue Atlantic Ocean
And the sunny beach in Portsmouth.

My box is modern and is made from granite, gold and wicker,
With jewels on the outside and jewels inside.
It is one of the most expensive boxes in the world.

Samuel Hayes (7)
Holly Lodge Primary School

Rainforest Destruction

The rainforest has a grey mist going through it.

The animals and insects are being trapped by fallen trees,
They are all angry and flattened by bulldozers,
Chop! Bang! Chop! Bang Chop! Bang Chop! Bang! go the axes.

Animals are angry,
The rainforest's death is close.

Joshua Girling (8)
Holly Lodge Primary School

My Story Box
(Inspired by 'Magic Box' by Kit Wright)

Into my story box I will put
A big blue whale swaying from the oceans
A big football rolling on the playground
And a Celt fighting a Roman on the field.

My box is shiny and made from ice
With dots on the outside and dragons on the inside.

It makes a roaring sound when you open it.

Zak McClounan (7)
Holly Lodge Primary School

My Scary Box
(Inspired by 'Magic Box' by Kit Wright)

The things I will put in my box . . .

The growl of a really big bear looking for some honey,
A big, black, hairy spider crawling up my legs
And a fat, yellow lion running after me.

My box is slimy and made from green frogs' eggs,
With animal teeth on the outside.
Inside there's a shark eating a fish.

Megan Joel (7)
Holly Lodge Primary School

Aircraft

Big jets, small jets, some no jets at all!
We are the monsters of the skies.
Carrying goods from cloud to cloud.
The noise we make is very loud.
Carrying you from country to country.
If we run out of fuel our engines will fail,
And we will crash with a bash!

Lyndon Weaver (9)
Holly Lodge Primary School

The Lonely Hamster

There was a little hamster,
Who was very lonely,
An alien jumped through the window,
And kept him company!

They soon fell deeply in love,
And the alien very kindly,
Got engaged to the lonely hamster,
And they soon got happily married!

Jessica Heritage (10)
Holly Lodge Primary School

Dangerous Jungle

In the thick green jungle,
With the swaying light green leaves,
The black monkeys swinging,
From tree to tree.

Rivers flowing rapidly,
Waves going by,
Tortoises swimming deeper,
Deeper than me.

Matthew Pearce (8)
Holly Lodge Primary School

The Big Beast

The big, bad tempered beast tears our ground apart, killing mud that gets in its way.
JCB should stand for a jealous criminal beast.

The grass under the tower of mud is screaming, 'Help, help!' and that's what the beast does.
It roars like the lions in the cage, trapped, no way to get out,
No wonder it makes those sounds.

Hope Rigden (9)
Holly Lodge Primary School

Ruined Rainforest

The strong sun shines,
Snakes slither silently,
Rushing river runs rapidly,
Rodents run ridiculously.

Creepy clouds come,
Cruel canes crash,
Mischievous monkeys moan.
Moody melons munch.

Charlotte Smith (8)
Holly Lodge Primary School

The Scary Mud Monsters

The big yellow beast starts crushing the earth with its big, giant claws.
One goes digging and the other one goes sleeping
And at the end a lovely, magical school.

Crushing and banging gives us very big headaches
Because we are the bulldozers and we work like mad.
So let's all give a big bang because we are the bulldozers and we work very well!

Alison Kenton (9)
Holly Lodge Primary School

Welcome To The Jungle

In the understory layer
Snakes silently, slowly, sneakily, slither
Down to pounce at its prey
Swallowing it whole in one go.

Monkeys swing high up above
Sheltered by the canopy of leaves
Up in leaves where no one eats.

Bradley Reed (9)
Holly Lodge Primary School

The Huge Destroyer

The destroyer came in and crushed our school ground,
It crushed and banged, and what was left went to the dump!

It scooped up and ate the ground
But if it is not hungry it goes into a huge castle of mud.

When the builders have a break
The destroyer grabs our toys and puts them in the castle of mud.

So the huge destroyer is *mad!*

Harriet Blackman (9)
Holly Lodge Primary School

My Unbreakable Box

(Inspired by 'Magic Box' by Kit Wright)

In my box I will put . . .
A melting snowman from the North Pole,
A football that will never puncture
And a fallen down tree.

My box is mouldy and made from copper wire
With bronze, sparkly sequins on the outside.
It has silver, dazzling bones in the corners.

Owen Foster (7)
Holly Lodge Primary School

Welcome To The Jungle

Snakes slithering, sliding and hissing down the jaguar's path slowly,
Hear the parrots mimicking you, they are lots of different colours.

The jaguar is jumping for its prey,
The lion's sleeping in its den.

The monkey's swinging branch to branch,
The crocodile swimming in the water
Frogs leaping in the water.

Jack Sargeant (9)
Holly Lodge Primary School

My Enchanted Box

(Inspired by 'Magic Box' by Kit Wright)

In my box I will put . . .
A snowflake from the darkest cloud in the universe,
The most valuable picture from the richest artist in the Milky Way
And a golden boot from Usain Bolt.

My box is classic and made from silver,
With ice on the outside and cobwebs in the corner.
It has an enormous spider crawling up the side.

Peter Kimber (8)
Holly Lodge Primary School

My Transforming Box

(Inspired by 'Magic Box' by Kit Wright)

Into my box I will put . . .
A first-aid kit in case someone hurts themselves,
Some ready-salted crisps in case I get hungry
And a very fast red and white car.

My box is shiny and made out of leather and marble,
With stars on the outside and fairies sparkling around inside.
It has butterflies peeping their heads out.

Ellie McDonald (8)
Holly Lodge Primary School

The Destroyed Rainforest

Lots of trees suffering
In the dull graveyard
All animals are calling out
In a wasteland
Now, sadly, animals don't have homes
Now all there is, is a symbol of horrible death
Animals extinct like the dinosaurs, finally.

Ben Austin (8)
Holly Lodge Primary School

The Magic Box

(Inspired by 'Magic Box' by Kit Wright)

I will put in the box . . .
The cry of the first baby,
The sight of crabs scuttling on the seabed.

I will put in the box . . .
A lovely taste of chocolate,
The beautiful sound of the wind whooshing,
The great smell of a burger.

Charlotte Mills (7)
Holly Lodge Primary School

My Secret Box

(Inspired by 'Magic Box' by Kit Wright)

In my box I will put . . .
My friends lying on me,
The good leaves falling off a tree
And the beautiful waves crashing side to side.

My box is ancient and made from ice,
With stars on the outside and magic inside.
It is as blue as the sky.

Becky Roberts (7)
Holly Lodge Primary School

Rainforest Animals

Slithery snakes hanging from twigs and leaves.
Cute monkeys sneaking and playing with their brothers and sisters.
Terrifying tarantulas crawling away to catch flies to eat for supper.
Scary centipedes under the ground looking for food.
Creepy crocodiles walking slowly because he's tired.
Tiny turtles in the ocean getting tangled in the seaweed.
Loving lizards washing themselves with their tongues.

Olivia Smith (8)
Holly Lodge Primary School

My Treasure Box

(Inspired by 'Magic Box' by Kit Wright)

In my box I will have . . .
The palm trees swaying from side to side in the air,
The waves moving gracefully on the sand
And the children making beautiful sandcastles on the beach.

My treasure box is sparkly and made from shiny jewels and gold,
With marble on the outside and fairies on the inside.
When you open it fairy dust comes out.

Maisie Elder (7)
Holly Lodge Primary School

Animals' Feelings

The emerald-green leaves shimmering
Some monkeys playing in the trees
But then down slowly and painfully
Big green trees sad, angry, scared they might be next
Animals angry and homeless.
The birds sad their eggs are destroyed
No chicks or becoming a mother
What will happen to the jungle now?

Megan Gallacher (9)
Holly Lodge Primary School

Puppies, Puppies

Puppies, puppies
Big, furry and strong.
Puppies, puppies,
Loud, short and long
Puppies are active, playful,
Crazy and cute too,
I love puppies,
Do you?

Georgia Williams
Holly Lodge Primary School

Destroyers

The monster diggers are fast or slow
They move carefully in the colourful dirt.
They dig up dirt to make a building
Yellow tractors smell of paint and oil.
They move like a turtle
Swiftly through the mud.
As fast as they can
Making a mud bath.

Isabella Kemp (9)
Holly Lodge Primary School

Rainforest Trees

The shiny, green leaves
The yellow logs
The brown branches
The rough bushes
The leaves are so pretty
The trees are skinny
The tall trees are nearly touching the sky
The sky is silver.

Benjamin Henden (9)
Holly Lodge Primary School

Jungles

Slidey snakes slithering through the jungle.
Crabby crocodiles creeping away.
Messy monkeys making cake.
Tabby turtles trotting.
Tigers taking turns playing tag.
Lizards licking their skin.
Tarantulas tread on ants.
Lions licking their food.

Charlotte Polley-Hughes (8)
Holly Lodge Primary School

The Mysterious Jungle

The slimy and fierce snake slithering up the scaly trees
Some dozy, black monkeys sleeping and squawking birds around them flap their wings.
The flopping water dropping down on the thin leaves, *splash, plank, splash, plank* everywhere.
Now hear the cats roar through the jungle.
See the deer swallow a big chunk of grass
Hear the bears walk *plop, plop, plop* all through the jungle.

George Brown (8)
Holly Lodge Primary School

The Shiny, Yellow Digger

A shiny, yellow digger grinding up the mud,
Scooping like a dinosaur,
Crunching the multi-coloured dirt with its talons,
Squashing anything in its way,
Smells of leaking petrol and oil,
Trots along like a monster truck,
Funny flicking up mud.

Callum Leppard (9)
Holly Lodge Primary School

The Bulldozer Bully

The immense yellow destroyer,
We call him the Bulldozer Bully.
He's the obliterator of our school
It swallowed up our sand pit and chewed on all our classrooms.
Then it fell drearily asleep
But then it was awake again and it crashed down on our classroom,
All it left was one abnormal, giant footprint . . .

Anna Lambert (9)
Holly Lodge Primary School

The Emerald Jungle

In the rainforest soft, black monkeys swing happily through the trees.

Birds squawk loudly as they fly freely through the jungle.

All the animals are fleeing in fright as their homes are destroyed slowly in the light of the sun.

Thomas Joel (9)
Holly Lodge Primary School

The Secret Box

(Inspired by 'Magic Box' by Kit Wright)

My box is a secret box
It has pink sparkles on top
Inside it has golden fairies
My box has gold and silver sparkles around the sides.

Louise Cocking (7)
Holly Lodge Primary School

The Huge Yellow Smasher

The big *smasher* destroys everything in its path!
The huge smasher moves like a *strong* elephant!
The *giant* smasher, smashes up all the mud!
The enormous smasher is *invincible!*

Matthew Charleson (10)
Holly Lodge Primary School

Rock

R unning around messing up the place
O n and on all over the place
C arrying it round the world all the time.
K issing all the girls I meet.

Chloe Hoare (10)
Holly Lodge Primary School

Hallowe'en Night

A boy was walking past a graveyard,
When he heard an eerie howl,
So he looked back and saw something foul.
He thought it was a trick and carried on walking,
But then suddenly he heard someone talking,
This was obviously quite scary
And not at all nice.
So he started to run,
When he saw some mice,
Whose teeth were as sharp as knives,
So he started to run faster and faster,
When he saw something even nastier,
A zombie was looming over his head,
And with a booming voice he said,
'Go home young child,
For it is Hallowe'en night,
Where you do not want to get a fright.'

Joshua Greensmith (9)
Kew College

Hallowe'en

At midnight on Hallowe'en,
When black cats' eyes glow green,
When ghastly creatures take over the sky
And witches on brooms come sweeping by,
When pumpkins grin, cackle and hiss
And the quietness of night you begin to miss.

When the cold wind comes blowing by,
When there's no silence in the sky,
You're all tucked up in bed at night,
When vampires come for a bite,
When you're in bed, they're out being sly,
There's more to Hallowe'en than meets the eye.

Cicely Helen Irwin (10)
Kew College

It's Hallowe'en

It's Hallowe'en tonight, what do you want to wear?
'As long as it's scary, I don't care!'

All I want to get tonight are glorious sweets
And don't forget about all those yummy, yummy treats!

Off we set all brave and bold,
We finally reach a door all silver and gold!

Knock, knock, knock, we patter on the door,
'Trick or treat?' we shout. 'We want more!'

Chocolate, candy, cakes and cream,
'We are the only Hallowe'en team!'

Hour by hour the sweets are eaten,
The lady who gave us them thought she was beaten!

The clock strikes 12, the witches are out,
Time to go home, no roaming about!

Sophia Hawkes (11)
Kew College

Hallowe'en Horrors

On Hallowe'en when the old man died,
Wolves howled and skeletons cried
Upon his sad burial night.
Witches with their cats took flight,
To do their evil deeds again,
Until their lives, too, reached an end.

Isabel Hawes (9)
Kew College

Hallowe'en Horrors

On Hallowe'en night,
Witches take flight,
With their cats,
On their laps,
Upon their brooms,
Over the tombs,
Where danger looms.

The clock strikes midnight,
Children take fright,
For monsters are in sight,
Tonight children run along the street,
Shouting, 'Trick or treat?'
But deep in the night,
The poor children will scream with fright,
For they will find their host
Is just a ghost!

Natalie Jade Kaza (9)
Kew College

Hallowe'en Horrors

Witches take flight
With their brown, warty cats
On their laps.

Vampires bite with their sharp, pointy teeth,
Women cry, so do men.
People running up the stairs
Get teeth dug into them.

Ghosts come out of their tombs,
Scaring people, did you see the ghost
Who drowned his slayer
And then threw him on a rock?

Pumpkins get their insides peeled,
Their faces get carved,
They really do feel warm inside
When danger is about.

Benjamin Court (9)
Kew College

Autumn

Leaves crunching like crisp packets under people's feet,
The glowing sun beaming down on a field of gold,
Crickets chirping as the grass gently sways.

Watch the sunset with shades of orange, red and yellow,
Slowly sinking into a deep pool of darkness,
As night creeps into the sky.

The gentle breeze scattering beautiful brown leaves
Around the silent orchard.
Foxes scurrying and sleeping round half naked trees.

Hedgehogs hiding away underneath the huge pile of leaves,
Snoring quietly as a mouse,
Moving only when eating a worm or stretching their tiny legs.

Lily Alexander (10)
Malden Parochial CE Primary School

Seasons

Summer:
Warming in the sun
Time to go and play outside
Find all our friends
Fill up the swimming pools
Turn off the taps
We're on a water meter

Autumn:
Frosty, chilly fun
Red, green, gold, yellow patchwork
The leaves off the trees
Lying on the ground
Being blown around the park
Fun to jump in them

Winter:
Wrap up in the snow
Fluffy balls fall from the sky
Nice and warm at home
Snowballs being thrown
Icy snowman in the cold
Water rushing off

Spring:
Plants all rising up
Poking out the moist soil
Flower beds are full
Lambs are in the field
Mint sauce on the plate for lunch
I like roast dinner.

Alexander Abbott (10)
Malden Parochial CE Primary School

Animals Of Taiwan And China - Haikus

It's black, white, black, white,
The cuddliest thing you've seen,
You have to hug them.

With happy faces,
They eat bamboo every day,
It's the cute panda.

A black and white tail,
They can climb up trees so high,
Big, round, yellow eyes.

They jump tree to tree,
They are as high as your waist,
The ring-tailed lemur.

Orange, white and black,
They live by the chilled river,
They are like big cats.

They like to ambush,
The cat has really big claws,
It's the quick tiger.

It is grey and white,
It will swim underwater,
They all have three fins.

They are nice to us,
They communicate so well,
The Yangtze dolphin.

Cameron Brown (10)
Malden Parochial CE Primary School

Marmite

Jump out of the cupboard
And land upon my toast,
Ready to be eaten,
Make sure you don't boast.

Marmite, you're my favourite,
Marmite, you're the best,
I love you, Marmite,
Because you're better than the rest.

It's brown and runny,
It's made of yeast,
In a big jar,
It's a scrumptious feast.

There's a champagne version
And one for cricket,
When your jar's empty,
Make sure you lick it!

When you're eating Marmite,
Don't spill it on the floor,
And if you're still hungry,
Ask for some more!

Henry McCallum (11)
Malden Parochial CE Primary School

As The Rain Sparkles

The rain pours down with its dripping sound,
It feels like tiny pinpricks as it hits my face,
With the sun desperately trying to peek through the clouds,
Suddenly sends a ray of bright light,
That feels warm on my face,
As I walk along I see droplets of water fall from leaves,
As they sparkle in the warm sunlight,
And then a beautiful rainbow appears.

Amie Leddington
Malden Parochial CE Primary School

My Dream Rocket

5, 4, 3, 2, 1,
I am going to have fun
Floating all around
Off the ordinary ground
Where nobody knows
Scarcely anybody goes
Out in the dark space
Nowhere is like this big place
All dark and lonely
So travel very slowly
It could be scary
You might hear the canary
But it should be fun
Near the scorching, summer sun
I'll never forget
My own *dream rocket!*

Eun-Young Jee (10)
Malden Parochial CE Primary School

Space - Haikus

Aliens playing
Mars being made of Mars bars
Saturn's ring spinning

Pluto shrinking down
The sun shining brightly round
Jupiter smiling

Mars rover roving
Satellites inspecting space
Venus sitting shy

Mercury boiling
Martians floating everywhere
Neptune singing songs.

Faiz Chughtai (10)
Malden Parochial CE Primary School

Killer Lion

It is super fast
It is super cuddly
But it is so strong

Be very careful
Pouncing out to kill its prey
Sprints to kill its prey

Faster than its prey
As silent as a mouse when it hunts
As big as two pigs
And can run really fast
It hunts by itself.

What is it?

Ryan Harrison (10)
Malden Parochial CE Primary School

Hallowe'en

Monsters everywhere,
Spiders in my dark, black hair,
Open if you dare.

Trick or treat tonight,
Witches on their magic flight,
Giving me a fright.

Mummies, ghouls and ghosts,
Standing under tall lamp posts,
Ogres making toasts.

So what have you seen,
On this spooky Hallowe'en,
Monsters are so mean!

Tia Hughes (10)
Malden Parochial CE Primary School

My Journey To Outer Space

Inky blackness,
Shooting star,
I wonder how many planets there are?
1, 2, 3, 4, 5, 6, 7, 8,
I think there are eight.
Wow, this is great, all around me,
As black as slate.
I think I'm going to land on the moon soon,
Zoom!
I'm on the moon,
Feeling floaty and light,
I have had an outstanding flight,
But now I must say goodnight!

Chloe- Albury (10)
Malden Parochial CE Primary School

Homework

I was asked to do a poem for my teacher,
Just didn't know what subject to pick,
It's all so very, very hard,
The time went so quick.

Still couldn't think what to do,
Maybe I'll just give up,
But then Miss Flynn will not be proud,
So I won't win the poem cup.

Finally I thought of one,
But by now it was getting late,
Oh please Miss Flynn, don't tell me off,
I have tried so hard that I have left my dinner on the plate.

Bethany Allchurch (10)
Malden Parochial CE Primary School

Christmas Morning

Children wake up in the morning
And find out Santa has come
Children shout, 'Hooray!'
Like they had just won the lottery.

Getting all those presents
There is nothing better than that,
Inviting your family round,
Getting fat.

Eating turkey and chicken,
Stuffing yourself with ice cream,
This is the best Christmas ever,
Just like a dream.

Sam Krzystyniak (10)
Malden Parochial CE Primary School

Crazy Kittens

C razy and fun,
R ats can run, but cannot hide,
A lways energetic,
Z oo animals have no chance,
Y owling at every turn.

K illing mice, rats and voles,
I n and out every chance,
T rees are my climbing frame,
T easing animals smaller than me,
E nergy never runs out,
N othing can stop me,
S leeping isn't an option.

Lucy Hallgren (10)
Malden Parochial CE Primary School

The Circus

Clowns jump around like lunatics,
Tightrope walkers fall off a bit.

Jugglers juggle with juggling balls,
Stuntmen do flips off the walls.

A lot of monkeys run like elves,
Lion tamers scare themselves.

Fire-eaters show off to the crowd,
The ringmaster shouts out loud.

People eat lots of candyfloss,
Bulls get impatient and very cross.

Nathan Molden (10)
Malden Parochial CE Primary School

Water Waving

Swooshing, swaying
Water playing
Dazzling in the night.

Meandering around rocks
As I stand there
And watch in my Crocs
And the water then turns right.

Sparkling, shining
Bubble finding
Fish with scales so bright.

Emily Tomlin (10)
Malden Parochial CE Primary School

Ghosts - Haikus

Don't wake up at night
Or you will get such a fright
And I'll make you shake

At night I awake
And rise up from the gravestone
Then I drift around

I scream haunting shouts
And I visit every house
In the nearby town.

Annabel Langdon (10)
Malden Parochial CE Primary School

Christmas Day - Haikus

Santa is coming
Once again with my present
We all shout hooray

Today is the day
All the children shout with joy
Families unite

Wake up together
All the children open gifts
It's the end again.

Zane Wasati (10)
Malden Parochial CE Primary School

The Whistling Wind - Haiku

The whistling wind it
Goes through the trees in the woods
As madly as you.

Max Maragh-Wood (10)
Malden Parochial CE Primary School

What Am I?

I am a nice snack
You would hear about me in space
I can be eaten
I will only go bigger if you make me.
What am I?

A: Galaxy chocolate bar.

James Thomas (10)
Malden Parochial CE Primary School

The Snow - Haikus

Snowflakes are falling
Onto the sparkling, rough ground
Children are playing

The snowmen are built
Snowball fights are on the go
Children having fun.

Jennifer Jenkins (11)
Malden Parochial CE Primary School

Weather - Haikus

Windy, wet, cold day!
Miserable people stayed!
A freezing cold day.

A hot, muggy day!
Miserable people stayed!
A boiling hot day.

Cillian Creedon (10)
Malden Parochial CE Primary School

Cupcake

I am yummy,
I am scrummy in your tummy,
I am different sizes and flavours,
It just depends on your tummy.
I can be pink, yellow and white,
But I will never make you blue.

Chloe Alicia Jackson (10)
Malden Parochial CE Primary School

A Smile

It sits quietly just under your nose,
Stand up tall and strike a pose.
Hold it up, don't let it fall,
Otherwise you'll look a fool.
Don't frown nor smirk, a smile will do,
Clench your fists and don't feel blue.

Madeleine Woodland (10)
Malden Parochial CE Primary School

A Delicious Snack - Haiku

A delicious snack,
You'll only find me in space,
I can get bigger.

Calum Garner (10)
Malden Parochial CE Primary School

Fireworks - Haiku

Bright and colourful
In the night sky, dazzling light
Bang, boom, swizzle, pop!

Sophia Baibars (10)
Malden Parochial CE Primary School

As I Rise To The Stars

As I rise to the stars where I belong,
I go through the improbably black hole.
As I rise to the stars where I belong,
I see the moon with Neil Armstrong's footsteps
And the American flag.
As I rise to the stars where I belong,
I see all the stars and the biggest star of all,
The babbling hot sun.
As I rise to the stars where I belong,
I see all the planets, Mars, Venus, Earth,
Mercury, Jupiter, Saturn, Venus, Neptune
And last but not least, Pluto.
As I rise to the stars where I belong,
I bounce about space with no gravity to pull me down.
As I rise to the stars where I belong,
I come out of the dark, dark, impenetrable black hole,
Floating around in the spooky air.
As I rise to the stars where I belong,
I make my way back to Earth, it's boiling hot
But it's the middle of winter.
There's definitely something wrong.
I take off all my layers and drop them in the snow.
I look at the sun very carefully
And then I look at the snow.
I figure out the answer - the climate's changing.

Sapphire Oot Timson (9)
Parish Church Junior School

The Haunted House

As I entered, the floor creaked,
The floorboards yelled with pain,
Then I extended my arm and reached,
For the nearest door.

The curtains drew themselves open,
As windows opened their sleepy, dusty eyes,
As the morning light appeared,
The whole house cries.

Cries echoed around the house,
The cobwebs tore and fell to the ground,
Across the ground skittered a mouse,
Searching for some crumbs.

Radiators groaned and droplets leapt,
As I came near the TV went beep,
Alarm clocks shouted their wake-up call,
Sofas stood up and went to the hall.

The water went plop as it landed in the pot,
Cartons of milk leapt like dancers,
Wind blew into the manky cot,
And the water ran out of the taps.

The water was a sea crashing on the sink,
The sink was a shore, cutlery was people,
People dived into the waves because they didn't think,
And the tide came crashing in.

The milk and the cereal played in the bowl,
A silver, shiny spoon clinked in the milk,
As the planks of wood stirred the spoon,
Cereal felt like silk.

I saw a shake, I felt a rumble,
I tasted poison, heard a roar,
As I ran I had a tumble,
Picking myself up, I scrambled to the door.

I fled out of the haunted house,
As far as I could go,
As I was as scared as a mouse,
I knew I would never come back again.

Chinonyerem Igwe (11)
Parish Church Junior School

Tamil Boy

I saw the face
Of a Tamil boy,
Living in a camp;
I sleep in a clean, warm bed,
But his is hard and damp.

I saw the face
Of a Tamil boy,
Peering through a fence,
While I am free to roam around
A world that's so immense.

I saw the face
Of a Tamil boy
With hollows round his eyes;
I have three square meals a day
And fish to make me wise.

I saw the face
Of a Tamil boy
And I felt deeply sad;
For he has lost everything;
Home, sister, mum and dad.

Still, I think about
That Tamil boy
And wonder what's become
Of a child that is so much like me,
But his future is so glum.

Esteban Lais Kumar (8)
Parish Church Junior School

Books

Books, books, I love books.
Fat books, thin books,
Even books on a bat,
Fact books as well as the ones
Which are not intact.
Books, books, I love books.
Story books or gory books,
I don't care as long as it is good.
I don't care who wrote it,
Even if it was written by a block of wood.
Books, books, I love books.
Adventure books, lecture books,
Paperbacks, hardbacks,
Even those with no back.
Books, books, I love books,
Books on wars, books on doors
And books on floors
And ones about walls.
Books, books, I love books.
New books, and books made of gold.
Books, books that I love,
All of the types above.

Daniel Apio (9)
Parish Church Junior School

World Peace

I wish, I wish there could be peace,
With violence at an end!
Where we could live in harmony
And parties never end!
Where hugs and kisses are the norm
With every boy and girl
And everyone was free to travel
Throughout this beautiful world.

Krystal D'Anjou (8)
Parish Church Junior School

Voice Of The Forest

At the crack of dawn, when the sun rises,
The birds start to sing,
The animals in the forest are the first to stir,
And the bees start to sting.
In the distance a bear growls, a squirrel squeaks
And a lone wolf howls,
Ravens, crows and sparrows scatter,
Badgers hide and squirrels scurry,
From a tree of sleeping owls.
Nocturnal creatures go to sleep for the night ahead,
Like foxes and bats.
As dusk falls, and the day-shift settle down to rest,
Come out, do they the dogs and cats,
Leaves rustle in the light breeze, that sway the trees,
Bushes and shrubs about,
Racoons, the pesky little thieves, come to steal junk,
Litter, leaves and nuts, oh what an amount!
At the crack of dawn, when the sun rises,
The birds start to sing,
The animals in the forest, are the first to stir
And the bees start to sting.

Harishon Sasikaran (10)
Parish Church Junior School

Autumn

A season of falling leaves
And hibernating trees
The mornings are cold, sparkly and misty
A season for crunching and munching
And chestnut roasting and crumpet toasting
For bonfire dancing in the midnight air
A season for listening and whistling
And children chasing leaves
That have fallen off the trees.

Vanda Emmerson (10)
Parish Church Junior School

The Dirty Streets

I got off the bus and played the game 'rushing home for tea'
With a hop and a skip I dodged some spit
With a bounding leap I miss the heap
Of disgusting smelly poo
Scraping my feet I avoided the pieces
Of reeking, splashy vomit
I stepped and I skidded
On a packet of empty crisps
Cans and cans rolled and stood blocking my way
Some were empty, some had plenty
I passed down an alley, the stench of wee
Swirled around me
I turned a corner and stubbed my toe
On garden waste hastily placed
Without care or attention
I walked through the gate and I'm happy to say
I'd reached my destination
The game I played meant
I couldn't look up and wave
As my mind paid attention to the dirty streets!

Leyi Mitchell (10)
Parish Church Junior School

The Outdoors

The stream of pure blue water, flows down the steep green hill,
Stopping only to rest where rocks agree.
The chirpy bluebirds flying with the colourful hornbills,
The brave, brisk hares, scurrying near the stream,
The leaves as green as grass, hanging off the trees,
The children sleeping in the sun having lovely dreams,
The squirrels planting acorns and quickly bringing seeds,
All together the people were removing sticky weeds.
The beauty of nature in the great outdoors,
Where animals roam free and children play on moors.

Nana Ampoma Addo-Kufuor (10)
Parish Church Junior School

The Black Horse

The black horse stands
All alone, isolated
From everybody around
Him no one to
Take care of him
No warmth, no
Home, nothing
His eyes are like
Shiny, black stones
His dark fur is
Like the beautiful
Night skies
He stands all by
Himself, as you
Pass him you see
All the fear in
His eyes and how
Afraid he is
Every day is the
Same thing, isolation.

Tania Jebbison (10)
Parish Church Junior School

Big, White Polar Bear

Big, white polar bear,
Soft, white ice-like fur,
Wanders far, wanders near,
On ice, on snow, with no fear.
He slips, he falls, nearly stumbling,
He's hungry, looking for food, belly grumbling.
His world's getting smaller,
Because of the gas we burn,
Soon he'll be gone, when will we learn?

Darcy Brown (8)
Parish Church Junior School

Creepy Camping

There is moonlight in the sky
My mouth runs dry
Stars twinkling bright
On this creepy night
Something is coming
Let's start running
Wet grass under my toes
Cold sweat running down my nose
Something is coming
Quick, let's run and hide
The pack's in sight
Let's make a dash under the slide
The night falls silent
Could it be a big, hairy giant?
Eyes closed tight
Waiting for a mighty fright
But what is that I hear?
A miaow, a cat
Casper is that you?
Oh it is. Fancy that!

Sophie Richardson (9)
Parish Church Junior School

The Morning Mist

As I walk down the path, a mist joins me,
It sneaks through my clothes and onto my skin.
It cools me down on hot mornings,
And warms me up on cold ones.
When the sun shines through it,
It will shine like a diamond lake.
If the rain comes, it will glisten and sparkle,
It always seems to brighten my day,
Even though it is a cloudy mist.

Luc d'Eca (10)
Parish Church Junior School

Victim

I uttered a soft cry
I won't tell anyone why
Her hand clutching my auburn hair
She tugged it hard.
Oh, how I wish I wasn't there
She dismissed me with her glance, stalked off
Her gang at heel as if in a trance.

And that's my life every day
Being crushed, stamped out
Bullied and tortured in every way
If they opened their eyes, then they would see
All the memories they've engraved in me.
And every time I try to explain
Tears gather in my eyes and creep down my cheek
I feel all frail and weak.
I want to speak, I try to tell
But my mouth stays silent, as under a spell
'Tell someone' the posters say
I may one day . . . one day.

Rebekah Elliott (10)
Parish Church Junior School

Limey Man

Limey man, the Bogey man he scares the creeps out of me
I see him, I smell him, what a terror for me
He's out at night, drinking and sitting
What a scared little me.

He's the one and only Limey Man of Bogey Land
And don't you forget it
He scents out little children
He waits in the shadow of your dark room
Then he strikes
Boo!

Nathan Hoskins (9)
Parish Church Junior School

The Forest Nights!

In the night the forest is alive,
I fail to see how I can survive.

The forest air whispers my name under its breath,
I shatter to answer this mysterious voice.
The air pulls me graciously.

The thick, tall tree trunk hunches over me.
Also the thin, stringy vines reach out to grab me,
As they glide upon the murmuring, murky breeze.

The lake sparkles like the glowing moon upon the horizons,
It could drift you away like a bird spreading its wings to fly.

Upon the ground the creepy-crawlies dance
Across the concreted floor.
Also at night the stony, lumpy ground rustles and leaps up
In the dark, pitch-black skies.

This is no ordinary forest at night,
But in the mornings it's ordinary and bright,
That's why it's called the forest night.

Shantel Jebbison (10)
Parish Church Junior School

Mysterious Cat

I prowl in the sunlight
I walk swiftly in the dark
But nobody hears me going to the park
I lick my lips viciously for the food that is yummy
But I lie down when my tummy is runny
I really like to go out when it is sunny
But when I pounce and bounce for my prey
This is what I say
'Miaow!'

Jada Macauley (8)
Parish Church Junior School

My Little Sister

My little sister is cute and small
And if you hold your finger out,
She will begin to pull.
My little sister gets very messy
And if she doesn't get her food quick enough,
She gets very stressy.
Sometimes she's happy
And sometimes she is sad,
But whenever she sees me,
She is always glad.
When she is alone, she starts to moan,
My little sister is very cheeky,
But when it is late, she gets very sleepy.
My little sister likes to pull my hair,
And when she goes to sleep,
She likes to cuddle her bear.
My little sister likes to spit out her dummy,
But whenever she is crying,
She is crying for her mummy.

Stephanie Hindle (8)
Parish Church Junior School

My Cat, Douglas

My Norwegian forest cat, soppy as can be,
Was found in the countryside behind an old oak tree,
He was taken to a shelter, luckily for me,
I was hunting for a cat that day and he was meant to be,
When we got him he settled in perfect as can be,
And soon he was a part of our loving family,
He really is a pickle and can be very, very daft,
When brushed, his bottom goes in the air and really makes me laugh,
He is really big and fluffy, this sums up my cat,
I love him very, very much and that, my friend, is that!

Cally Olliver (9)
Parish Church Junior School

When I Grow Up

When I grow up
I think I'll be,
A sailor sailing
The seven seas,
But if that doesn't quite work out
I'll have to be,
A pig with a snout,
But as I don't really want to be that,
I'll be a fireman
Wearing a hat
But I don't want to be burnt real bad,
So instead I'll stay at home, going mad
But that doesn't sound appealing to me
So I might as well
Make friends with a bee
But all of that doesn't matter right now,
Cos at the moment
I'm milking a cow!

Bethany Hatcher (9)
Parish Church Junior School

The Classroom

This is quite a nightmare
Like a cup and a spoon
You think you're a smarty pants
But you just smell like poo.

The boys think they're fast
The girls think they have brains
But anyway the teacher's such a pain.

The deputy is teaching us
And telling you it's true
It's all about poetry
But I'm writing this to you.

Kerris Redway (9)
Parish Church Junior School

The X Factor Judges!

I love watching the XFactor,
Although some of them sound like a tractor.
Cheryl likes the good-looking guys,
But when they sing bad she says goodbye.
And now we come to Simon,
He's very nasty and rude
And his trousers are really huge.
Then of course there's Danni,
She is an Aussie babe,
I wonder what will happen to her
When her looks start to fade.
And last, we come to Louis Walsh,
I think if he sang on X Factor,
He would sound like a horse.
Now I start to finish,
I hope you know a lot,
And I will let you into a secret,
I think Simon *is hot!*

Rachel Hewett (9)
Parish Church Junior School

In My Attic

In my attic we keep everything
A door, a boat, anything
A box of broken books
Some horrible crooks
Some broken pencils
And even some stencils
A broken shoe
Some slimy goo
Don't go up there
You might get eaten by the bear
(Hiding behind the water tank)!

Ethan Barnes (10)
Parish Church Junior School

The Tomb Of Doom

I'll tell you a story
You may find it gory
It's about a mummy
You'll be screaming for your dummy.

I stood in a tomb
It's called the Tomb of Doom
It's old and webby
Just like my old teddy.

It shouted at me
I needed to pee
It didn't let me go to the loo
I didn't know what to do.

It told me to clean up
And so did my pup,
So it wasn't a tomb
It was just my bedroom!

Samuel Hayes (9)
Parish Church Junior School

The Secret Garden

Nails of grass whirl in the wind,
Their bodies always tend to shiver and grin.

The windows stare,
Fences try to bare.

Dustballs roll by,
Lonely and bored,
Dustbins flinch.

Fences bare their height and feet,
The grounds of the garden loom out of sight.

The people on the swings swing higher and higher,
Not knowing that they were as high as jet plane flyers.

Ali Younis (10)
Parish Church Junior School

Thailand

Arriving in Thailand on the aeroplane,
Daddy took us to our house.
A dog called Jay was barking,
Friends Boom and Beem were waiting.
Lighting candles in the temple,
The smell of incense in the air.
From the top of Buddha Hill,
We could see everywhere.
A beautiful hotel for sleeping,
Steaming soup noodles for eating.
A deep blue pool for diving,
My daddy's Mercedes for driving.
The golden temple in Bangkok,
With marble tiles that gleam.
Every night I go to sleep,
Thailand is in my dream.

Christopher Luala (9)
Parish Church Junior School

Autumn

I love autumn because acorns
And leaves fall from the trees,
I love autumn because
It's warm.
I think autumn is new life,
Autumn leaves are as yellow as gold
And they fall from the trees faster
Than a pencil dropping.
Autumn is happy
Autumn breeze is warm
And never too cold.
But beware, the cold breeze of winter
Is coming.

Dylan Akhawais (10)
Parish Church Junior School

I Remember . . . I Remember

I remember the plane high in the sky flying,
With the excitement of the holiday coming.
I remember sun-scorched, golden beaches with majestic castles,
Holding back the tides with endless battles.
I remember the hot sand dunes under my feet burning
And the races to get to the top running.
I remember the waters, warm and soothing,
While out in the ocean swimming.
I remember the hotel, standing tall and coloured brown,
In the middle of Playa Del Ingles town.
I remember the seagulls calling,
While effortlessly in the sea diving.
I remember nights walking peacefully,
Around the brightly lit resort with my family.
I remember missing Gran Canaria hugely,
Stepping on the plane regretfully.

Deepesh Patel (9)
Parish Church Junior School

Winter Mayhem

W inter is a time for fun and joy
I cy cold girls and boys
N o T-shirts and shorts
T ime for jumpers and coats
E verybody wrapped up tight
R eady for a snowball fight

M aking snowmen
A nd snow angels
Y oung and old have some fun
H appy Christmas everyone
E xpecting Father Christmas to come
M y favourite time of year!

Ella Dunn (9)
Parish Church Junior School

Look At Mariama

Look at Mariama, as she cries in the night,
While I snuggle into bed and hold on tight.
She sadly prays for some bread while I happily munch instead,
Look at Mariama as she shivers in the cold,
While I play with my silver and gold.
All she longs for is a bed, while I selfishly rest my head.
Look at Mariama as she has nothing to drink,
While I barely just stop and think.
She has no one, no one to love,
While I have my mum staring full of love.
Look at Mariama, she's so different, unlike us we're all the same,
She has nothing, she has no one,
We have everything, more than one.
Look at Mariama, it's so hard to believe,
She lays there full of grief, full of agony, full of pain,
For us this is just a game.

Mary Aysel Allahverdi (10)
Parish Church Junior School

Hallowe'en

Hallowe'en is coming,
A night the children fear,
There are monsters, bats and witches
That suddenly appear.
Screams and growls fill the black night air,
Someone's knocking on the door,
I wonder who is there?
I slowly open the door
To see who could be standing in the street.
Suddenly, a scary voice shouts out,
'Trick or treat?'

Connor Robertson (7)
Parish Church Junior School

Ballet Shoes

My heart is pumping like never before,
My mind is embracing.
I feel free.
My legs can express themselves
While I pirouette,
But sometimes I do fret.
As I do allegro work,
I'm flexible and warm.
I can do anything.
My tutu is a fairy sparkling with passion
And expression.
My ballet shoes dance around,
Guiding me like I'm a dog,
By keeping my place in line,
Because here I am safely dancing,
Feeling I'm fulfilling the destiny of my life.

Khadijah Hayden (10)
Parish Church Junior School

Winter Days

Winter is coming up and I can't wait until it snows!
The winter will be freezing cold.
Snow will fall down from the sky, just like a feather falling softly down.
Winter, winter, winter, winter,
I love the sparkly, soft snow,
I can throw the freezing cold snowball on my sister,
We would have so much fun!
Cold, cold, cold,
I would sit by the fire to keep nice and warm,
After that I would be brushing my teeth,
Snuggle into my comfy bed and off into my winter dream!

Yuki Kan (10)
Parish Church Junior School

Sea, Sun And Life

You see the sea rising, then falling against the hard, ragged rocks
That scratch the deep, clear sea.
After the seagulls scan the air for food,
The angry sea like a lion pounces on the coast,
Trying to flood the land.
But its attempts are feeble as it crawls back slowly,
Swiftly and silently like a snake,
It calms down for seagulls to feast.

You see a star bright in the cold-eyed sky,
Lighting the day and guarding it like a king.
Blazing and shining its unmerciful rays of heat,
Beating on the creatures of Earth.

We see light, rain, snow and life living
Onto the end of time and life.
Living, breathing and seeing everything in life.

Martin Niimoi (11)
Parish Church Junior School

The Haunted House

The neighbourhood kids had wagered their bids,
To see if their dare for me to go in there
Would give me a scare!
Then I crept into the haunted house,
I soon found myself stepping on a mouse,
I started to think that this bit of a lark
Would be better performed not in the dark!
The final straw was hearing a lion roar
From behind a wooden door.
I got a terrible fright,
So I ran off into the gloomy night!

Callan McLennan (11)
Parish Church Junior School

My Sweet Dream, Brighton

The day I went on a trip to Brighton with my family,
I heard the white seagulls screeching
As if they were singing a little tune.
The different shaped shells whispering
The sound of the waves into my ear.

The time I walked onto the Brighton pier,
I felt very excited to see around it
And go on rides at the funfair and have fun.
I did not want to go home
Because I had never got uncomfortable or fed up.

I visited the Sealife Centre
And saw all different kinds of lovely fishes,
Swimming around the cylinder we were in.

I wish to visit this lovely place again!

Berfin Bedir (10)
Parish Church Junior School

The Haunted House

In screaming woods and empty rooms,
Or gloomy vaults and sunken tombs,
Where dusty floorboards creak and decay
And shadows dance at the close of day.

Where bats feed on the wing
And ghostly choirs on winds sing,
Where swords of ages old in battle clash
And shimmering shades of freedom dash.

Kirsty Northwood (10)
Parish Church Junior School

Autumn

Autumn is the time of year where the world changes colour,
From green earthy tones to orange brown and red.
Autumn's leafy coat is the most beautiful sight,
While the trees' hair falls onto the warm coloured ground.

Swallows arrive dragging autumn with them.
The crisp leaves crunch under the feet of everyone.
Hiding the green grass from view,
Not to be seen until the cold winter.

The air at autumn is blustery and windy,
The sky as light as the sun.
Acorns and conkers parachute off trees,
At early hours light fades into dark.

As people tidy their gardens, leaves dance away in the wind.
Everything is quiet now, but winter is nigh.

Jasmin Daley (10)
Parish Church Junior School

The Haunted House

The cracks in the windows, the broken-down fence,
The overgrown garden so high and so dense,
Cobwebs in corners, squeaking doors,
Running rats and creaking floors,
Light shines through a broken shutter,
The dusty staircase so full of clutter,
A sudden bump makes my heart jump,
A chilling scream, wakes me from a terrible dream.

Freya Griffiths (10)
Parish Church Junior School

Whale

I once had a whale,
Who had such a wail,
She was loud,
Which caused a crowd,
She smelt of sea perfume,
Then we had to vacuum,
She made such a mess,
So we went west,
There we found another,
A brother and a sister,
I'm telling you guys,
Even in the skies,
Having a whale,
With such a wail,
Is hard work!

Tayla Danaher (10)
Parish Church Junior School

Untitled

Music is a gift from God.
Music helps us to communicate feelings which we cannot express.
Music tells stories.
Music can make you happy or sad.
Music is the food for the soul,
Music crosses race, age or colour.
Music connects us all and makes us one.
Music is the language of love.

Barucha Bentsi-Enchill (10)
Parish Church Junior School

My Teacher Mrs Tinwell

My teacher is fantastic.
My teacher is special.
My teacher is sporty.
My teacher is humble
And exciting to be with.
I love my teacher for caring about me.

God bless my teacher.

Ezra McDonald (9)
Parish Church Junior School

Flowers

Flowers can be big, flowers can be small
Flowers can be colourful, look at them all.
There are shiny sheets of daffodils in the field,
While sunflowers are looking over the rainbow
After the summer showers.
Flowers can be big, flowers can be small,
Flowers can be colourful, look at them all.

Samuel Oliver-Rowland (10)
Parish Church Junior School

Winter

W ild wind rushing through our hair,
I n the frosty, chilly weather we play all day,
N oticing the white, puffy snowballs dropping,
T rickling snowflakes tumbled up together,
E verywhere's covered in tiny white crystals,
R ivers frozen all icy and smooth.

Anton Iwaniuk (8)
Parish Church Junior School

The Blitz

Be aware people
The Blitz is coming
Be aware of the explosives
The war is coming.
Loud and long sirens
Everywhere there's an
Alert.
The war is here
There's continuous
Sound.
For a year the war
Didn't start.
But a year later
She awakens
Once again.
Scared like another
Time.
Air raids are starting
The war is still going again.
Most buildings are gone
The heart of her is still standing
Upright!
Where am I?
Who are you?
'I'm trapped' nowhere to go
I can't move
The Blitz is here
Does it show?
But I'm the city of London!

Robert MacDonald (10)
Purley Oaks Primary School

Untitled

Relieved and relaxed,
Speechless,
Tranquil,
Proudly adoring her
Children.
Suddenly!
Mighty explosions!
Ear-blasting.
Wailing of her wounded children,
Dying.
Endless sirens wailing.
Revolting smoke.
Breathes in the acrid smoke,
Poisonous acid,
Choking her,
Knotting her lungs up.
Harmful smoke,
Fire blazing through her
Body.
People are fading.
What will London do?
And the taste!
The taste going through her mouth,
Choking her.
She feels hotness going up
Her arms and legs.
She feels hot going up her.
London is dying.

Yasmin Basith (10)
Purley Oaks Primary School

I Am . . .

I am as graceful as a golden eagle,
Soaring majestically over the Himalayan mountains.
As swift as a peregrine falcon at top speed,
Clutching the rabbit with my huge talons,
I get it indeed.

Handsome as a male bird of paradise,
Calling the oh so brown but beautiful female to mate.
Beautiful as a male monarch butterfly,
Travelling far and wide to find a lovely lady friend.

I am faster than a yellow spotted cheetah,
Hunting for prey,
Ready to pounce on my lunch today.
I'm as active as a kangaroo bouncing across the land.

As beautiful as a bright red rose,
Picked from a colourful flower bed.

I smell like purple lavender
Picked from a healthy, green field.
I smell like juicy fruit and berries from the country.

I sound like an orchestra playing their songs and instruments
Peacefully in the open air concert.
I sound like a sweet, blue canary,
Singing a song in the break of dawn.

Abinayah Rathakrishnan (9)
Purley Oaks Primary School

I Am . . .

My touch is soft, you couldn't feel it at all,
And even if you did, you would get a tender feeling.
My hand is so smooth and slippery,
It's like a polished glass window.

I move like a princess,
Walking slowly and carefully as if I am one.
As graceful as a pony galloping freely
Across the summery moor.

I am as magnificent as a glittery butterfly
Shimmering in the light blue sky,
Cute as a kitten, pretty and fluffy,
Sleeping in a pink, frilly basket snuggled up tight.

I smell like a white chocolate cake fresh from the oven,
With melted chocolate and Smarties on top.
I smell as sweet as a daffodil that just bloomed,
With the smell of Heaven, fresh air and strawberries.

My voice is gentle and light,
It sounds like an angel singing in the sky.
It is sensitive and beautiful,
Like the sound of the butterfly wings.

Olivia McKenzie (9)
Purley Oaks Primary School

May I Never Be Forgotten

Heart torn to pieces
Hair as spiky as a hedgehog's
Fire burning through her skin
Eyes as dark as a cave
She will never be forgotten
As she walks with pain
She cries with tears
She will become strong again.

Junior Zziwa (11)
Purley Oaks Primary School

I Am . . .

As fast as a cheetah chasing its prey,
Ready to strike for my dinner today.
I am as graceful as a swan,
Gliding freely across sparkling water.

I feel like fur on a fluffy sheep,
Smooth and warm walking across fields,
As smooth as glass hard and rigid,
In my spot doing nothing in my space.

I look like a gym instructor teaching football,
Tall and fit, ready for my next lesson.
As long and skinny as a sausage dog,
Walking and jumping for a stick.

As loud as an elephant stamping through the rainforest,
Looking for a cave for safety.
As loud as a tornado spinning loud as a hundred cars
Beeping and waiting for a rest.

I smell like a fresh orange picked from a tree,
So sweet and ready to put in the shops.
I'm a cake, smelly and tasty on a plate,
For a party for children today.

Khallid Muhammad (9)
Purley Oaks Primary School

The Blitz - London Cries

Relaxed, tranquil,
Speechless, complacent.
Bored, calm,
Caring for her children.

Ear-blasting explosion,
Crumbling bricks
From the mighty
Boom!
'Stop the wailing!'
Sirens squealing,
Boom! Boom!
Poisonous smoke,
Clogging her lungs,
Infectious gun powders,
Catching her throat,
Destroying her lungs.
She sees her children
Collapsing.
Her eyes filled with tears.
She has seen a dreadful sight.

Christine Kancel (10)
Purley Oaks Primary School

I Am . . .

I am as playful as a dancing kitten,
As sweets as a singing lark,
As clever as ABC,
Like a graceful, swaying swan.

I am as proud as a feathery peacock,
As buzzy as an angry bee,
As good as glittering gold,
As soft as a white cloud falling.

Mariah Green (9)
Purley Oaks Primary School

London Cries

Lost in herself,
Drowned by the cold and the darkness.
Her world and children
Lost!
Wherever you go
People crying, lonely with
Lust
Self consciousness, an empty
Heart
Lay deep inside of her waiting to
Explode with
Tears.
As she watched her home
Burn with fear, although
Her world will be
Forever in her memories
It fades slowly with her town.
Now she is trapped, can she escape
From her dark, black heart?

Kyra Lord-Lindsay (10)
Purley Oaks Primary School

I Am . . .

I smell delicious like a ripe, red apple with juice
That runs down my chin when I bite it.

I am beautiful as a colourful, red rose
Picked from my garden and displayed all over the country.

As soft as a blanket washed with Daz
And left to dry in my garden.

The sound I make is like Beyoncé,
Loud and wonderful, she sings like a diva.

As fast as a cheetah running to catch its prey.

Mercy Nyathi (9)
Purley Oaks Primary School

Destruction In London

Once still and quiet
Then the ground began to shake.
Her heart began to race like the engine of a plane.
It felt like it skipped a beat.

1,000 degrees fires burning
The reflection in her eyes
The smell of powdered brickwork
The sound of bombs dropping
Her screech made the windows shatter
Into a million pieces.
Her house crushed
Her body filled with rage.

She was motionless
The planes flew overhead
The second bomb fell on the docks.
She prays for peace
After a while there was silence.

Shoamar Best (9)
Purley Oaks Primary School

Help, I'm Trapped By Smoke

Please get me out
My eyes are burning
I see the whiteness of smoke
Help! Help!
My beating heart beats like a hammer
Banging on the door
I am scared I might faint
Then someone walking in smoke
Shocked one of my children has survived
Excitement
I am strong
I can fight bombs!

Zafirah Javed (10)
Purley Oaks Primary School

The Blitz - London Cries

Reaching tall,
She happily lives,
Her children play until that day.

Bang! Bang!
Bombs screeching down.
Scared and petrified,
She rapidly awaits,
As the pitch of grey smoke rises.
She watches her children battling for their lives.
Bombs thundering down,
The effect pulling her down.
Buildings crumbling to her feet.

Struggling to fight back,
She pushes her way up.
Her children will succeed,
Win the battle.
She will wait until that day comes.

Tyron Sonko (11)
Purley Oaks Primary School

I Am . . .

I'm as adorable as a beautiful butterfly
Glistening in the deep blue sky.
Charming as a velvety, textured, bright red rose
Smelling like a juicy, red strawberry.

I sound as delicate as an angel in Heaven,
Above clouds as smooth as paper swifting in the sky.
Attractive like a hummingbird sitting straight and proud,
Watching fish swim by.
I sound as sweet as a soothing lullaby,
Being sung quietly to a sleeping baby.

Tania Zama (9)
Purley Oaks Primary School

Shattered Memories

Silence.
Confusion.
Eyes lit up
From the flames.
Hearts pumping
Louder than explosions
Going off!
All memories shattered
In different piles.
Sweat pouring
From the heat.

To be honest
She is relieved
That the almighty
Bombs have
Stopped,
But not for long . . .

Daniel Allen (10)
Purley Oaks Primary School

London

Darkness, danger everywhere,
She turns tiredly around
Woken by the undulating sirens.
Falling like a drunken lady.
She hears something dropping quickly.
Rattling crazily
Hearing children screaming
On her streets.
The smoke puffing like a man smoking
On her streets.

Charntelle Kennedy (10)
Purley Oaks Primary School

I Am . . .

As fast as a spotty, yellow cheetah,
Ready to bite for my life.
As jumpy as a brown monkey,
Swinging through the long vines.

I am smelly and sticky,
Like sweets from a shop.
Brown and yummy,
Like a big fat cookie.

I am beautiful as golden sand,
People tread on me like I'm a rubbish can.
I'm beautiful as a lovely red rose,
Getting picked from the bushes.

I sound like the wind,
Swishing slowly through my beautiful garden,
Sound like hot fire,
Blasting through my house.

Shamia Matin (9)
Purley Oaks Primary School

I Am . . .

I am as sweet as a singing lark,
Like a graceful, swaying swan,
As playful as a dancing kitten.

I am as proud as a colourful peacock,
As fresh as a plain white daisy,
Like a shining sun.

I am as gentle as a sleepy lamb,
As white as a snowflake falling,
Like a soft, puffy cloud.

Liah Fossum (9)
Purley Oaks Primary School

London's Dark Days

Blinded and petrified
A mist of smoke drifted around
Catastrophic destruction
Undulating cries of pain when her children crumble.
Excruciatingly painful
Her heart pounding in her sorrow
This once majestic wonder now fallen.
She falls.
The ground shakes with a terrible quake
She screams.
It echoes.
The windows shatter.
Trapped!
Doesn't know what to do
Then suddenly regains strength
Her head up high once again.

Zuhair Faisal (10)
Purley Oaks Primary School

The Memories Of London

Bombs are falling
She is motionless and hushed
All around the ground shakes
But she is bold and lifeless
Bombs have dropped
Blazing fire, almost 1,000 degrees
Her heart missed a beat
Where are her children?
Silver slivers of glass smashed
Memories intact for that won't change
She knows that they will go soon
And it will be noiseless
Again!

Ryan Searle (11)
Purley Oaks Primary School

London

The huge city standing
With his pride
Looking at his children
Screaming for their lives.
The fog so thick that he can't see
The noise like thunder
Screaming in his ears.
Nearly falling over
Fighting for his life.
Sixty thousand dead,
Who he cannot save.
Tears in his eyes,
Heart beating like a drum.
Cannot run anymore,
Cannot sleep,
Waiting for it to end.

Djamel Zekkar (11)
Purley Oaks Primary School

London Cries

In her eyes you can see
Disappointment.
In her heart she whispers,
'There's hope!'
But still there is doubt all over.
Her heart turns to dust as she discovers
What has become of her.
She bows down and cries.
She feels herself getting restless.
She is quiet and hushed.
She can hear the air raiders coming,
She is terrified!
She doesn't know what to do.

Olivia Bell (10)
Purley Oaks Primary School

The Bad Day

Her hair is curly
Heart pounding faster than a cheetah
Blazing smell of dust up her nostrils
Hot fire coming out of her mouth
Mighty explosion
Smoke coming out of her ears with outrage
As she lies, the earth starts to shake
When she shouts the window breaks
She's torn into pieces as she cries
No hope, no hope in her life
She looks at the crushed houses
Statues and bookshelves
Few remain
Danger everywhere
But she survives.

Anita-May Crawford (10)
Purley Oaks Primary School

London Terrified

Darkness, danger everywhere she turns,
Something is falling dangerously fast.
All sirens go off like mad solves.
People, children screaming for their lives
As they go into the shelters.
Suddenly, a gigantic explosion happens!
All over London in one blink of an eye,
All she can do is watch in horror,
Seeing all of her helpless children
Dying so quickly.
She is getting angry, wishing it was all over.
Her life and children,
In the hope
That Britain will win the war
And quickly.

Megan Searle (11)
Purley Oaks Primary School

London Cries

Trapped and scared
Planes zooming around her
Screaming like she's lost it
The Germans just keep bombing her
But she still tries to stand strong
Until they get to her heart.

Catastrophic things are happening
All around her
But she tries her best to stay up
She succeeds
By blowing away all the planes around her
She doesn't know where she got the strength from

She did it, all the planes
Have really surrendered.

Michael Omekowulu (10)
Purley Oaks Primary School

Fight To The End

The blazing fire shoots out like a rocket,
But she stands,
Her heart shattered to pieces
Like the explosion of a volcano.
But she stands.
She falls on the ground
Like an earthquake exploding.
Her hearts flows like a dragon,
Her heart is burning.
The firefighters gliding
Like skateboarders jumping.

Finally, the war ends.
She is getting confidence.
Now she and her children are free!

Anish Mahesan (10)
Purley Oaks Primary School

I Am . . .

I am as proud as a peacock,
With my vibrant feathers held high,
Where I stand I look and stare,
As happy as a sweet, singing lark.

As large as life can be,
I look up and down
With the bright, burning sun
Shining on me.

Natalia Russell (9)
Purley Oaks Primary School

I Am . . .

I am as good as glittering gold
I am as quiet as a whispering mouse
I am as freezing as snowy ice
I am as gentle as a playful lamb.

I am as smooth as velvet silk,
I am as sweet as honey,
I am as soft as white clouds,
I am as fresh as a beautiful daisy.

Shannon Hedley (9)
Purley Oaks Primary School

The Magic Box

(Inspired by 'Magic Box' by Kit Wright)

I will put in my box . . .
The tears she always cried and the smile she always had,
The wonderful things we did together,
Her bright blue eyes on her beautiful face.
Her eyes made the sky brighten up even more.

I will put in my box . . .
All the adventures we explored and the times we had,
Her laugh she did when I did something funny
Just made me smile and think of the times
We could have had together.

I will put into my box . . .
The poems she always made and told me,
The funny voices she always did when she had to say them,
The rhymes she had and the rhyming words,
I just loved them and loved what she did.

I will put into the box . . .
The memories we shared
And the fun we always had together,
Whatever they were good or bad,
I will always remember you wherever you are
And wherever I am.

My box is fashioned from her eyes and her sunny smile,
The lid has all the adventures on it,
All the memories are in the corners.
Its hinges are made by her
Personality and secrets.

I shall surf in my box
In a magical world on a magical island in the colourful sea,
With the sunset beaming down on me.
The reflection on the water is just beautiful like you
And that is how I will remember you.

Gemma Barlow (11)
Whyteleafe Primary School

The Magic Box

(Inspired by 'Magic Box' by Kit Wright)

I will put in my box . . .

The tallness of a troll, the magic of a fairy,
The wisdom of a wizard and the danger of a dragon,
The legendary laugh of an ancient goblin.

I will put in my box . . .

The softness of the snake's slimy skin,
The enormous elf,
The pulsing beat of the magnificent giant mushroom.

I will put in my box . . .

The sharpness of the shark's teeth,
The bulldozing head of a bull
And the alien's mouth as wide as an avalanche.

I will put in my box . . .

The rage of a ghostly ghoul
And the power of the mighty pig's snort,
What about the loudness of me and my brother arguing?

My box is created . . .

With all the colours of the rainbow
The hinges will be made of the colossal galaxies,
Little planets
And the sapphire-blue of the Chelsea badge.

I shall fly away
To these faraway places
And meet all these creatures and do all these things
And at the end we will all have to say goodbye
And listen to each other cry.

Robbie Roper (11)
Whyteleafe Primary School

My Magic Box

(Inspired by 'Magic Box' by Kit Wright)

I will put in my box . . .

The blinding ashes of an erupted volcano,
The hot magma of underground hotness,
The hot, boiling lava at the summit.

I will put in my box . . .

The deafening sound when it erupts,
The hot heat of the wind
And the jagged peak on top.

I will put in my box . . .

The dribbling magma going down the big rocks,
The killing smoke when the lava dribbles onto the ground,
Where I was standing.

I will put in my box . . .

The merciless rocks spitting from the top,
Pounding the ground below,
Smashing the trees and houses.

My box is fashioned from gold
With hot colours of the volcano
On the sharp rock's edge.

I shall explore in my box
The true beauty of nature
At its most ferocious power,

The colour,
The sight,
The sound,
The fear.

Alexander Hayes (10)
Whyteleafe Primary School

All About Me And My Heroes

I love to sing and dance
Even though it's very hard
I love to work with animals
Although they bite and scratch you!

I love to do some gardening
With my strong dad
I love to do some cooking
With my beautiful mum!

My sister is amazing
She can play the flute
I love to play music
I can play two instruments!

My granny is amazing
And so's my grandpa
My aunties love me so much
And so do my uncles too!

I have a pet goldfish
My sister has one too
I wish I could get a dog
But my dad's too allergic.

I have loads of friends
They're all so nice to me
I have a few cousins
They all love to see me!

I hope you enjoyed this poem
But as you can see
It's over
I hope you enjoyed it as much as me!

Alexandra Dobbs (10)
Whyteleafe Primary School

The Magic Box

(Inspired by 'Magic Box' by Kit Wright)

I will put in my box . . .

The fluff of my dog
The height of her silky ears
The care and attention she gives us.

I will put in my box . . .

Her beautiful bark in the morning
The crazy running around after Mum winding her up
The time she stole my giant lolly.

I will put in my box . . .

Her rounding up chickens, guinea fowl and ducks
The wag of her tail on her first Christmas
Her woof when you say, 'Harry'.

I will put in my box . . .

The faces of the scared golfers
The car chasing
The happy smile she gives us
When we come home from school.

I will put in my box . . .

A Jakalope on the run
A flying dog
A flat shell tortoise.

My box is fashioned from gold and diamonds
With a ruby dog on top.
The hinges are made from golf clubs.

I will run with my dog in my box.

James Hardy (10)
Whyteleafe Primary School

My Magic Box

(Inspired by 'Magic Box' by Kit Wright)

I will put in my box . . .

The day she jumped out at me from hiding in a box
The day she lay on my lap sleeping

I will put in my box . . .

The day we took her to the park
And she jumped and played
She ran round and round and chased her tail

I will put in my box . . .

The day we lost her at the park
And found her sleeping by the car

I will put in my box . . .

The silk of her black and white fur
The way her tail would wave
As I walked through the door

I will put in my box . . .

The loud bark she had
And how it deafened us all

I will put in my box . . .

The day she passed away
And left us

My box is golden and silver
And has a bronze picture of her on the top
The hinges are made of stars
That she would bark at.

Oliver Morris (9)
Whyteleafe Primary School

The Magic Box
(Inspired by 'Magic Box' by Kit Wright)

I will put in my box . . .

The brown, dangly fur of my dog
The colour of his rough paws
The lighter brown of his ears
And the loud cries
And the protection he always gave me.

I will put in my box . . .

The sharpness of his uncut nails
The glistening white of his teeth
With his soaking nose
And his love
And his happy times with me.

I will put in my box . . .

His long tummy with the look of a sausage
With his big, broad muscles
And the pointiness of his face.

My box is fashioned . . .

With the dark brown colour of his skin
A picture lies on top of the box
With his smile
Its hinges are made out of his baby teeth
With stars round the edge.

I shall play with my dog in my box
In the green of the fields
And will stroke him until I die.

Cameron Cudlip (10)
Whyteleafe Primary School

Geographical Places

(Inspired by 'Magic Box' by Kit Wright)

I will put in my box . . .
A fiery red core as hot as the sun inside a volcano,
A mountain, almost vertical,
A pool of lava bubbling like a boiling kettle.

I will put in my box . . .
A waterfall cascading into a lake of pure water,
A sudden drop of the cliff at the top,
Water glistening in the sunlight.

I will put in my box . . .
A green forest facing the plains of Africa,
A brave baboon swinging in the treetops,
A tall tree standing out from the rest.

I will put in my box . . .
The tall tips of a range,
The rocky rage of the jagged sides,
The bare, sharp outcrop of a mountain.

My box is fashioned from volcanic rock,
Wood and water from a glacier.
The hinges are made of solid gold
With all my memories and thoughts inside.

I shall look inside my box
And explore all the crevices of the world.
I will think of all the living creatures,
All the different landscapes
And all the different buildings,
Landmarks and pollution we've made.

Tom Anderson (11)
Whyteleafe Primary School

The Magic Box
(Inspired by 'Magic Box' by Kit Wright)

I will put in my box . . .

The first bike wheel I had,
The handlebars I gripped tightly when I went down a steep hill,
The super, silver shade of my bike.

I will put in my box . . .

Snow from a snowy mountain,
The wood from a snowboard,
A black ski mask.

I will put in my box . . .

The six strings from my guitar,
The picks I played my guitar with,
The amplifier I plugged my guitar into.

I will put in my box . . .

My favourite basketball,
The first shot I scored,
My wicked basketball boots I used.

My box is built from wood and silver,
The lid will have all the things I wrote about,
The corners will be gold bent snowboards.

I will use my box for racing, skiing, scoring baskets
And playing the guitar.
I will use my box a lot
And it will never be forgotten about.
That's my box.

Rick Owens (10)
Whyteleafe Primary School

My Magic Box

(Inspired by 'Magic Box' by Kit Wright)

I will put in my box . . .

The last video I ever played,
The cave-like colour on the case,
The analogue stick on the controller.

I will put in my box . . .

The memory card that saved my games,
The blueness of the PS2 sign,
The rumble of the hard drive.

I will put in my box . . .

The first game I ever got,
The sound of a gun firing in Call of Duty 3,
The voice of Jak II.

I will put in my box . . .

The moon from a night-time setting,
Kong from the video game,
The roar of a Kawasaki superbike.

My box is fashioned from
Metal, 99 calibre bullets
And a picture of Halo the futurist army man
With a green Kawasaki superbike on the lid
And Kong's teeth for the hinges.

I shall ride my K794 round Silverstone in my box
Into the misty distance.

Charlie Michael Carroll (10)
Whyteleafe Primary School

My Magic Box

(Inspired by 'Magic Box' by Kit Wright)

I will put in the box . . .

My hamster, Hidey,
How she always wanted to play
And lick people's hands with her little tongue.
How I remember she had fudge-colour fur
And her little fluffy tail sticking out.
Most of all, her eyes used to shine in the sun every day
And how I loved her so much from my heart.

I will put in the box . . .

How her nose used to pop up out of the bed.
When she was younger, she was half the size of your hand
And always struggled to get up the little pipes in her cage
And slide all the way down again.

I will put in the box . . .

Hidey, she was always sleeping
And when I took her out of the cage and felt her bed,
It was lovely and hot.

I will put in the box . . .

Every time we used to watch a film
I could always hear her little wheel squeaking,
So I had to move her.

My box is fashioned with love
And I will always remember Hidey right in the middle of my heart.

Megan Parker-Lowe (10)
Whyteleafe Primary School

The Race

Yesterday we made paper planes,
Mine was made out of paper
With flames on the side.
I love it, though I won't like tomorrow.

Next morning was the day,
Races all the time,
Everyone was shouting and screaming,
But I was just standing there in the enormous line.

Ready, go! Miss Green blew the whistle,
Sarah and Molly got up first.
Molly's paper plane went the furthest,
Sarah's just sat in the middle of the hall.

Next was me,
I was against Eric,
My legs were shaking,
Sweat was pouring down my face.

Ready, go! Miss Green blew the whistle,
Eric has flown his, now it was my go.
Up it went into the air, then *splog!*
It fell right in front of my feet.

The teacher wasn't looking, I had a chance.
Shuffle, shuffle, I moved it on with my feet.
It went a little further, but still no difference.
Halfway it travelled, but no more than Eric's!

Sophie Spall (10)
Whyteleafe Primary School

My Magic Box

(Inspired by 'Magic Box' by Kit Wright)

I will put in my box . . .
My dog, Buster, who passed away
Every time his sloppy tongue licked me
I had a good feeling.

I will put in my box . . .
Every time I saw his face
He gave me a smile
He was my best friend.

I will put in my box . . .
When I played with him all the time
He will always be there in my heart
I miss him a lot.

I will put in my box . . .
When I was in the park
When I was a baby in my buggy
As my mum pushed me along
Whoever tried to get near me
He would bark.

I hope he is alright wherever he is.
I love you, Buster.

I wish in my box . . .
I wish to spend one more day with him in the park,
Playing with him and giving him one last cuddle.

Matthew Weller (10)
Whyteleafe Primary School

Magic Box

(Inspired by 'Magic Box' by Kit Wright)

I will put in my box . . .

The first time I ever stroked
Her fluffy, soft skin.

I will put in my box . . .

The first time I ever held the tight new,
Shiny lead for her.

I will put in my box . . .

The day we sat at the table
Trying to decide what to name her.

I will put in my box . . .

The day I went to the park with her
And heard her beautiful bark.

I will put in my box . . .

The day I came back home
And she faded away.

I will put in my box . . .

The tears that I had, but you licked them off,
Even though you weren't there.

And my box will be made out of the sadness that night
When I went to bed.

Callum Bassett (10)
Whyteleafe Primary School

The Magic Box

(Inspired by 'Magic Box' by Kit Wright)

I will put in my box . . .
The speed of a whirlwind,
The heat, fire and anger of a volcano,
Spitting rock from its peak.

I will put in my box . . .
The spinning waters of a whirlpool,
The mass destruction of an earthquake,
Tearing down major cities.

I will put in my box . . .
The deathly cold of the tallest mountains,
The icy waters of the Arctic Ocean,
Holding mighty icebergs.

I will put in my box . . .
A freezing blizzard blocking roads,
The burning deserts of Africa,
And the danger of the Amazon jungle.

My box is styled from . . .
The molten rock of a volcano,
The ice of a mighty iceberg
And its hinges are made from jagged rocks of a mountain.

In my box I shall climb the tallest of mountains
And ride the winds of a tornado.

Cameron Skeet (10)
Whyteleafe Primary School

The Magic Box

(Inspired by 'Magic Box' by Kit Wright)

I will put in my box . . .

The deadly cats of Egypt,
The deadly dogs of Africa,
The deadly turkeys of Turkey!

I will put in my box . . .

The oceans full of magnificent sealife,
The ancient fish of the world,
The giants of the sea,
The kings of the oceans - the sharks.

I will put in my box . . .

The exciting theme parks,
The wonderful ancient temples,
The giant forest lands.

I will put in my box . . .

The bloodthirsty Dracula,
The hideous werewolf,
The ancient beast called Gollum.

My box is made of . . .

The rare gold of Egypt,
Wood from a faraway land.

Joseph Hawkins (10)
Whyteleafe Primary School

My Magic Box

(Inspired by 'Magic Box' by Kit Wright)

I will put in my box . . .
My ambitions and my dreams.

I will put in my box . . .
My past and future.

I will put in my box . . .
My hopes and fears.

I will put in my box . . .
My friends and family.

My box is fashioned from gold leather,
Sprinkles of stardust scattered on top,
The hinges are filled with shine from the sun.

In my box,
I shall fly through my memories,
I shall read my dreams like a book
And I shall surf through my treasures,
Scanning each and everything from my box.

And last of all, I will put in my box,
The things that mean something,
The ones you can never lend,
Love, friendship and family -
The things that will never end.

Sophia Carey (10)
Whyteleafe Primary School

My Magic Box

(Inspired by 'Magic Box' by Kit Wright)

I will put in my box . . .
The fur of my dog's hair,
The sparkle of her collar
And her funny smile.

I will put in my box . . .
The softness of her paws,
The sharpness of her claws
And her fluffy little legs.

I will put in my box . . .
The wetness of her nose,
The long, thin shape of her beard
And her black, shining eyes.

I will put in my box . . .
The funny way she walks,
The weird way she holds her toys
And the sadness when she has done something wrong.

My box is made of cuddles, kindness and love
And also the colour will be pink and covered in love hearts.

I shall travel with my dog
And go to all her favourite places
With her sparkle dog collar and lead to match.

Isobelle Woodman (10)
Whyteleafe Primary School

The Football Box

(Inspired by 'Magic Box' by Kit Wright)

I will put in my box . . .

The memories of winning my first game with my team,
I will put pictures in of my best coach,
I will put my old football kit in the box.

I will put in my box . . .

When we only needed to win or draw,
I will put in the memories of becoming the league champions,
When I got a trophy, I will put that in the box.

I will put in my box . . .

The tears from when my coach unfortunately died,
I will put in the memory of my friends on the football team,
I will put my friends and best friends on a piece of paper
And put the ashes in the box.

My box is made from glass and gold,
With my picture of my coach,
With rock and gold hinges.

I shall play football in my box,
On a massive football pitch
And whenever I hear the ball hitting the net,
We will all shout, *'Goal!'*

Archie Merrett (10)
Whyteleafe Primary School

My Magic Box

(Inspired by 'Magic Box' by Kit Wright)

I will put in my box . . .

The gallops we shared together,
The awards we won together,
The memories of our past.

I will put in my box . . .

The sweet smell of his morning feed,
The beat of his smooth canter,
The brushes I groomed him with.

I will put in my box . . .

His old, worn out horseshoes,
Hairs from his beautiful tail,
The sparkle in his deep brown eyes.

My box is made from wood
With gold trimming around the edges,
The hinges are made from strong steel,
The front has a picture of him on it
With stars all around.

I will travel in my box to Epsom racing stables,
To enter competitions to win prizes
And become an equine champion.

Eloise Kitchener (10)
Whyteleafe Primary School

My Magic Box

(Inspired by 'Magic Box' by Kit Wright)

I will put in my box . . .

My secrets I like to tell to my brother,
My sister and all of my cousins.

I will put in my box . . .

All of those times with my family
And all of those times together
Will go in my special box.
My box is made of all sorts of jewels
And fake, shiny diamonds.

I will put in my box . . .

All of those times when we went out
And had so much fun together.

I will put in my box . . .

My family and me going to a nice, beautiful place
And enjoying ourselves.

I will do in my box . . .

Some of my fun things I like to do with my cousins.
I will paint portraits of my cousins
And my cousins will paint one of me.

Sakina Hussain (10)
Whyteleafe Primary School

Magic Box

(Inspired by 'Magic Box' by Kit Wright)

I will put into my box . . .

The skin of a roaring lion
The first cat
A dog's first bark

I will put into my box . . .

The scales of a thick python
The scales of a goldfish
The spikes of a pufferfish

I will put into my box . . .

A shark's first tooth
The eyes of a tiger
The speed of a male cheetah

I will put into my box . . .

My first pet
The weirdness of some animals
The creep of a tarantula

My box is styled with animals from the world
This way I am never lonely.

I shall play in my box in years to come.

Charlie Arthur (10)
Whyteleafe Primary School

Cheese Dream

I had a dream,
A wonderful dream,
About an amazing world of cheese.

Big and small,
Yellow and white,
I danced and danced to show my delight.

But then it happened,
I saw my mother,
My dad, my cats and my stupid brother.

They used their powers to ruin my dream,
I couldn't defeat them,
Not with an army of cheese!

I had to think fast,
Faster than light,
I couldn't give up or I'd give up the fight!

But then something happened,
I couldn't see,
All I could hear was 'Get up Sophie!'

I opened my eyes,
I could finally see,
I was at my school and it was half-past three!

Sophie Webb (9)
Whyteleafe Primary School

The Magic Box

(Inspired by 'Magic Box' by Kit Wright)

I will put in my box . . .

The sapphire eyes of Dumbledore when he died,
The dark mark from Bellatrix Lestrange,
The agonising pain from Harry's scar.

I will put in my box . . .

The hatred from Professor Snape,
The malicious grin of Draco Malfoy,
And of course, the last remaining horcrux from Lord Voldemort.

I will put in my box . . .

The Felix Felicis that makes you lucky,
The Elixir of Life to make you live forever,
The Polyjuice Potion that changes your body into someone else.

My box is fashioned with moonstone,
Its hinges are made from Nargles' teeth,
The lid is made from Sirius' cosy, black fur.

I shall travel to the world of witchcraft and wizardry,
To explore Hogwarts, meet new friends,
Drink Butterbeer and play Quidditch with a broom.
I will also see Slytherin, Hufflepuff, Ravenclaw and Gryffindor.

Bo-li Chung (10)
Whyteleafe Primary School

The Magic Box

(Inspired by 'Magic Box' by Kit Wright)

I will put in the box . . .

The red, roaring blood of a lion,
The beating heart of a deer,
The wiggly washy giraffe's tail.

I will put in the box . . .

A fish's rough scale,
A shark's pointy tooth,
And a pearl.

I will put in the box . . .

A soft, silky feather from a bird,
A long, sharp beak of a pelican,
The scary head of an eagle.

My box is made of feathers and gold and pearls
With teeth of different animals and fish and birds.
Its hinges are pelican beaks.

I will surf in my box.
I will fly in my box.
I will explore in my box.

Jake Bentley (10)
Whyteleafe Primary School

Metal Detector

I am a metal detector and I'm very clever
Because when I beep it might be treasure.
You'll need a trowel to scrape away
A thousand years of Earth's decay.
What will you find? Some Saxon gold
Hidden in the ground so cold?
A Roman sword, a Celtic braid?
Or just your grandad's broken spade?

Madeleine Trubee (9)
Whyteleafe Primary School

The Magic Box

(Inspired by 'Magic Box' by Kit Wright)

I will put in my box . . .

My puppy's bark,
My nan's blackberry crumble and its smell,
A steam train with its steam.

I will put in my box . . .

My grandad's MG and the stuff to fix it,
The hurricane at my auntie's wedding
And a sunset in Spain.

I will put in my box . . .

A pet human and a hamster as its owner,
A frog that can't jump
And the 25th hour of the day.

My box is made of jelly with silence in the corners
And noise in the middle.
The hinges are made of children's laughter.

I will rock climb in my box,
Ride roller coasters in the centre of the sun
And eat apple pie the size of the Eiffel Tower!

Danny Hills (11)
Whyteleafe Primary School

Kitty O Kitty

Kitty O kitty,
How soft is your fur?
Kitty replies, 'Silky, I purr.'
Kitty O kitty,
Why do you lie right by the door
On a summer's night?
Kitty replies, 'I'll freeze to death
And I will die.'

Grace Leighton (9)
Whyteleafe Primary School

The Magic Box

(Inspired by 'Magic Box' by Kit Wright)

I will put in my box . . .
The happy times that me and my brother have had
And the photos of us smiling and scrapping,
Then lock the box up and hide it in my room.

I will put in my box . . .
The fun times me and my mum have had
And the memories we have had supporting and shouting at each other,
Then lock the box up and hide it in my room.

I will put in my box . . .
The joyful times me and my dad have had,
And the pictures in my head we have had laughing and loathing,
Then lock the box up and hide it in my room.

My box is made of wood
And decorated with stickers and photos,
Which are of us all together and some individually
And on the lid it says, 'Only open with the credit card'.

I shall keep in my box the key to the back door so I can go out
And look in the box in the shed so nobody can see me.

Tom Sussemilch (10)
Whyteleafe Primary School

Friends

Friends, friends, they're everywhere
They're always playing truth or dare
Some are happy, some are sad
Some of them, just plain mad!

Friends, friends, they tell good jokes
Some about folks, some about ghosts
But the only thing I like about friends
Is that your friendship never, ever ends.

Tanis Godden (10)
Whyteleafe Primary School

My Magic Box

(Inspired by 'Magic Box' by Kit Wright)

I will put into my box . . .

The softness of his fur coat
All the cuddles and strokes I gave him
And the roughness of his little pink tongue.

I will put into my box . . .

When he lay in his basket
Purring like a sweet little cat
And the afternoon he ate my fish.

I will put into my box . . .

His razor-sharp teeth biting into me
The thickness of his claws
And the day I came back from school
And my mum told me he was gone.

My box is silver with a picture of me, Lulu and Kovu,
It is decorated with hearts and stars.

I will see my cats in my box
And give them a great big hug!

Chapelle Cooper (10)
Whyteleafe Primary School

My Little Hamster

I have a hamster in my room,
His hair feels like a little broom.

My little hamster is so very cute,
But I do wish I could put him on mute.

He wakes me up in the night
And gives me quite a big fright.

But all in all my hamster is cool,
And he always wins when we play pool.

Kyle Boyce (10)
Whyteleafe Primary School

My Magic Box

(Inspired by 'Magic Box' by Kit Wright)

I will put in the box . . .
All my hopes and dreams.

I will put in the box . . .
Chocolate chip cookies
That melt in your mouth
And crumble in your throat.

I will put in my box . . .
Money and gold
Silver and riches
Shining brightly in the box.

I will put in my box . . .
My nan's homemade apple pie
The rich smell sends me into a thought of wonder.

My box is made of all those sweet things
Love, friendship, things that never end
My box will always be there with me
Even when I die.

Leah Barden (10)
Whyteleafe Primary School

My Magic Box

(Inspired by 'Magic Box' by Kit Wright)

I will put in my box . . .

My favourite hamster, Splinter
When I made him his very own ball car
So he could lose lots of weight
Because he was very fat.

I will put in my box . . .

My dog, Zeus because he was very fluffy
So I used him for a pillow
But his legs went funny and wobbly.

I will put in my box . . .

My favourite reptile, Collin my iguana
He was very calm
And once I went to bed
He was there on it fast asleep.

My box is made
With all the pictures of my animals.

Wesley Beard (10)
Whyteleafe Primary School

I Will Put In My Box

(Inspired by 'Magic Box' by Kit Wright)

I will put in my box . . .
A volcano erupting
The speed of lightning
And the sweetness of grass
The wetness of water
And the power of a tornado.

I will put in my box . . .
The sun and the moon
The sparkle of the stars
And the height of a mountain.

My box is made from . . .
The sparkle of stars
And the brightness from the sun
And the lid is made from the moon.

As I lift my lid of my box
A tornado will pull me in
And take me to another adventure.

Jake Faulkner (10)
Whyteleafe Primary School

The Magic Box

(Inspired by 'Magic Box' by Kit Wright)

In my box I will put . . .

The deadly orang-utans of the Amazon
The crazy golf of America
The nose-chattering smell of Swiss cheese

In my box I will put . . .

The dead birds my cat got to
The time I surfed a 20ft wave
And my face at the time

In my box I will put . . .

The memory of my stories.

My box is made out of chocolate
And guarded by flying pigs
With ice cream spears
And guard dogs with cheese.

My box is crazy!

Tomás Flynn (10)
Whyteleafe Primary School

My Magic Box
(Inspired by 'Magic Box' by Kit Wright)

I will put in my box . . .
When I touch their silk soft fur
Their noses twitching
Their cute grins
When I am covered in their fur

I will put in my box . . .
Their sharp claws scratching me
Their happy smile when they get their food
When I see them bunny hop
Their angry faces

My box is made of solid gold
And coated in memory metal
It has a picture of them on it
We shall play in the box together
And have fun together
I am talking about my rabbits,
Buzz and Bertie.

Angus Collins (10)
Whyteleafe Primary School

My Box

(Inspired by 'Magic Box' by Kit Wright)

I will put in my box . . .

The times we laughed and played
The way she laughed at me
Her funny laugh.

I will put in my box . . .

The things she did with Mum and me
The soft touch of her hand
The way she talked.

I will put in my box . . .

The number of times she cried in my arms
The place she loved to go
The times she said, 'I love you'.

My box is made
With pictures of me and you with love hearts
I shall play all day with you in my magic box.

Eden Henry (10)
Whyteleafe Primary School

Brussels Sprouts

They are nasty,
All the kids cry when they see them,
They are worse than carrots,
They are worse than cabbage.
I am obviously talking about Brussels sprouts
And don't get me started about spinach!

You can smell them from Russia,
Just as bad with celery
And don't get me started on spinach!

They're big, they're bulgy, they're full of badness,
They're little green balls of death
And don't get me started on spinach!

I hate them,
You hate them,
Even my dad hates them.
My little brother cries when he tastes them.
Don't get me started on *Brussels sprouts!*

Matthew Rook (10)
Whyteleafe Primary School

In My Magic Box

(Inspired by 'Magic Box' by Kit Wright)

I will put in my box . . .

The love I never shared,
The bracelet you wore,
Your first ever grey hair.

I will put in my box . . .

The necklace you gave me,
The tears that you cried,
The memories we shared.

My box is fashioned with silver and glass
With diamonds on the edges
And a picture of me and you.

I shall die with the box
All the way up to Heaven,
Holding it in my hands
All the way up to the sky.

Chloe Foster (10)
Whyteleafe Primary School

Sunshine

I've got sunshine in my bedroom,
I've got sunshine on my wall,
I've got sunshine on my pillow,
I've got sunshine on my stool,
And when I look outside, I smile at the sun.

We've got sunshine in the classroom,
We've got sunshine all at break,
We've got sunshine in the sky,
We've got sunshine in space,
But at night-time I say . . .

'Rise and shine, *please!*'

Bo-yan Chung (9)
Whyteleafe Primary School

The Magic Box

(Inspired by 'Magic Box' by Kit Wright)

I will put in my box . . .

The tears I never saw him cry
The ring he always wore
One of his smooth, grey hairs

I will put in my box . . .

The memories we shared
The presents I gave you
The love you gave me

My box is made of brass and glass
On it a picture of you and me
The hinges, gold, an amazing colour

I shall ride to the heavens in the box
To see you every day
And we can play
And watch the sun go down.

Annie-Louise White (11)
Whyteleafe Primary School

My Magic Box

(Inspired by 'Magic Box' by Kit Wright)

I will put in my box . . .

My baby brother's little tears
And his little hugs he gives me.

I will put in my box . . .

The little curl of hair and his little smile,
His chubby cheeks, they are soft and small.

I will put in my box . . .

The little hands and feet he as got,
They grip onto your finger.

I will put in my box . . .

His little knees.

I will put in my box . . .

The little cheeky smile he gives me.

Megan Christian (10)
Whyteleafe Primary School

Miss Hatherly

M y teacher is warm and cuddly
I could not wish for anyone better
S he talks to me every day
S he listens to me when I speak

H aving the best teacher makes me smile
A ny time I said I was sad she held my hand
T oday when I said I was scared, she told me I would be OK
H er smile makes me feel safe
E very time I told her I had been hurt, she said it would stop
R ainy days she would play hangman with me
L inda is her name
Y esterday she wasn't my teacher anymore and that made me sad.

Charlotte Olivia Newman (9)
Whyteleafe Primary School

The Magic Box

(Inspired by 'Magic Box' by Kit Wright)

I will put in my box . . .

My niece's drawings
And her writing and her first smile
And her DVD and her laughter

I will put in my box . . .

Her emotions and her TV
Her fun and her memories

I will put in my box . . .

Her tears and her first tooth
My box is made of cardboard
And it has her pictures
All around the box

I shall fly in my box
Travel to Scotland for two weeks.

Martin John Kearney (10)
Whyteleafe Primary School

The Magic Box

(Inspired by 'Magic Box' by Kit Wright)

I will put in my box . . .

The ink that an octopus sprays
And the sword of a swordfish
And a slimy, sticky piece of seaweed

I will put in my box . . .

A tooth of a shark
A piece of coral
And a bucket of seawater

My box is made of wood
And painted in the pattern of a clownfish
The hinges are made of fishes' fins

I shall swim in my box
And explore the underwater world
And creatures that live there.

Charlie Durrant (10)
Whyteleafe Primary School

I Will Put In My Box

(Inspired by 'Magic Box' by Kit Wright)

I will put in my box . . .
My fishes' scales and my gerbil's fur.

I will put in my box . . .
The time my mum put the gerbils on my bed
To get me up.

I will put in my box . . .
The time my gerbils bit me,
But I'll always love my gerbils.

I will put in my box . . .
The time I gave my gerbils my food.
I gave my fish fish food.

Nicholas Proudley (10)
Whyteleafe Primary School

True Beauty

What is true beauty?
Is it in the eyes of others?
Is it in one's appearance?
Or is it in the words we say?
True beauty shines from inside out.

True beauty my mum says
Is one's attitude shown to the world.
Sometimes it can be confused with appearance and riches,
But true beauty can never be bought or sold.
True beauty shines from inside out.

True beauty is in one's character.
True beauty when demonstrated, encourages
Honesty, kindness, friendship and love.
Beauty is like a picture with many beautiful colours,
True beauty shines from inside out.

Lily Alicia Shobo (8)
Whyteleafe Primary School

Gone Nuts!

I woke up this morning
And found myself yawning.
I went downstairs and saw cereal everywhere,
I walked in the living room
And saw my mum jumping off the walls
And saw my dad who was freakishly tall.

I walked in the garden to see my dog, Spike
And see him rolling around on the ground with delight.

I walked into school and saw Mrs Right
And to my surprise, she was flying a kite.

I don't know what happened today,
But I hope somebody can cast these nutty illnesses away!

Ellie Down (10)
Whyteleafe Primary School

Cheese Puffs

Fluffy little orange thing
Gives you a little zing
Also has a bit of bling

Let the cheese melt in your mouth
You are bound to shout out
'Cheese puffs!'
Then you will have a little zing
You will call everything a thing

Orange and yellow
Makes you bellow
But makes you smell like cheese
Then you go on your knees.

Ethan McCheyne (10)
Whyteleafe Primary School

My Hero

He rescued my rabbit from under the skip,
He helped me when I had a bad hip,
He saved me from the dragon's nip,
Who is my hero?

He saved me from the dog's claw,
He stopped me from falling to the floor,
He stopped me from crying more and more,
Who is my hero?

He always fights the terrible and bad,
He also fights the really mad.
So who is my hero?
My dad!

Emily Victoria Russell (10)
Whyteleafe Primary School

Swimming Race

Heart pounding,
Snakes slithering about in my stomach,
Knees knocking together,
Get Mum to help put my ruby-red hat on,
Adjust my goggles,
Go to lane four and stand on block,
Everything goes silent,
'Take your marks.' *Bang!*

Splash!
And I'm off!
So far I'm 3rd,
Coming up to the wall,
Swiftly doing a tumble-turn pushing off the wall,
Perfectly streamlined.
Yippee! I've overtaken someone.
Pace yourself Maia, pace yourself.

One more length,
'Come on, you can do it!'
I hear my coach, Tina shout.
Turning on to sprint mode,
Nearing the person in front,
Getting so tired, but I have to carry on.
Now we're level,
So I'm pushing myself that little bit extra,
Bam into the wall,
I'm aching all over,
But I don't care,
I've won!
The cacophonous noise of the crowd gets louder,
When they find out.

Maia Cooper (11)
Woodlea Primary School

Donuts

Donuts are good,
Donuts are pud,
Donuts are sweet,
Donuts are neat,
Whatever you want to find.
Some have icing,
Some have jam,
Some have beef
And some have ham.
Some are fluffy,
Some are flat,
Some look like a bowler hat.
Some of them have lots of cream,
Some of them are a delectable dream,
Some are sour,
Some are sweet,
Some have names,
This is Pete.
Some are strange,
Some are nice,
Some have mustard,
Some have rice.
Some are great,
Some are bad,
Some are good,
Some are mad.
Donuts really fill your tum,
Eat some more, it'll sag your bum,
Maybe a need to give my friend,
Some donuts that will never end!

Matthew Fendt
Woodlea Primary School

The Football Match

Beep goes the whistle
We've started
Suddenly the ball is played to me
He skids 1, 2, 3, 4, 5, goal!
Yeah!
Suddenly they're running through
Only keeper to beat
Hits the post
Shoot
What a save
It's a corner
Crossed in
They score
But no - it's offside

Half-time whistle
We are 1-0 up

They start
Long shot
Wide
Hits the ice cream van
I can almost taste the ice cream from here
Lovely
Creamy
I'm hungry
Quickly the ball lands at my feet
Pass, pass, pass, shoot - goal
We score
Final whistle
We win!

Daniel Moat (11)
Woodlea Primary School

Seasons

Spring:

Spring is the time when babies are born
Spring is the time to see a fawn
Spring is the time when all leaves are green
Spring is the time to eat some ice cream
Spring is the time to cycle your bike
Spring is the time to go for a hike

Summer:

Summer's the time for no clouds to be out
Summer's the time when there's often a drought
Summer's the time for the sun to be bright
Summer's the time to fly your kite
Summer's the time to jump some big waves
Summer's the time to explore dark caves.

Autumn:

Autumn's the time when the leaves all turn brown
Autumn's the time for them all to fall down
Autumn's the time to harvest the corn
Autumn's the time to mow your green lawn
Autumn's the time for Bonfire Night
Autumn's the time for a Hallowe'en fright.

Winter:

Winter's the time when it gets very cold
Winter's the time for warm clothes to be sold
Winter's the time when the snow covers the ground
Winter's the time to hear a Christmas sound
Winter's the time when Christmas is here
Winter's the time to see a reindeer.

Jack Wood (10)
Woodlea Primary School

Werewolf

Beware, beware of the werewolf,
My heart is thumping like the start of a race,
I stop,
I listen,
Argh!

Beware, beware of the werewolf,
It's there - the werewolf,
The werewolf is a pouncing tiger,
Waiting for its prey,
I stop,
I listen,
Argh!

Beware, beware of the werewolf,
Angry, hairy werewolf,
I think there's no way to escape,
I keep running as quick as lightning,
I stop,
I listen,
Argh!

Beware, beware of the werewolf,
The vandalising, cold-blooded werewolf,
I'm cornered,
He's got me,
It's the end,
For me!

James Surallie (10)
Woodlea Primary School

The Last Cross Country Race

Eating my snack in the car
Mum wishing me luck
Now I'm even more nervous
We've arrived
I see all my friends waving at me
Expectations are high
We line up
Jostling for position
Heart pounding
Nervous butterflies inside me
Breathe deeply
Bang! I'm off!
Pound! Pound!
My feet cover the ground
The mud starts to ooze
Into my shoes
Pound! Pound!
My feet cover the ground
One person ahead
My legs feel like lead
Pound! Pound!
My feet cover the ground
The finish line in sight
Run, run for my life
My final sprint
I have won!

Amy Dobson (10)
Woodlea Primary School

Hallowe'en

It's coming
The scariest time of the year
Hallowe'en
Demons, goblins
Giants and petrifying banshees of the jet-black night are out

Vampires are flying in their bat form
Sucking your blood as red as
Gleaming hot fire

Zombies are marching down the pavement
Like
Soldiers at Buckingham Palace

Ghosts as white as
Freshly cleaned bed sheets
Hovering around

Werewolves out
By the shimmering
Full moon
Howling

When all this scaring is over
All these spooky monsters
Will go back
Until the next
Hallowe'en.

James Davidson Grear (8)
Woodlea Primary School

Rainbow

What is at the end of the rainbow?
Who knows until you see.
What is at the end of the rainbow?
It might be a magic key.
Maybe it's a treasure chest,
Or a path to another world.
What is at the end of the rainbow?
All might be unfurled,
Maybe a land of unicorns.
Imagine a planet of sweets!
What is at the end of the rainbow?
A giant mountain of treats?
Perhaps a wild jungle,
With delicate emerald leaves.
I'd like to go to the end of the rainbow.
I hope everyone believes.
What is at the end of the rainbow?
Elves, pixies and fairies or
Goblins, witches and trolls?
All those magical creatures
And maybe living dolls.
All those people wonder,
What there could be,
But nobody knows for certain,
We will have to wait and see . . .

Eleanor Taylor-Pierce (9)
Woodlea Primary School

Caterpillar To Butterfly

Caterpillar wriggles its unsightly, horrifying bulk,
Like an alien from another planet.
Mouldy green, bristly,
An eyebrow with legs.
Munching and crunching its way
Through innocent, lush, green plants.
Devouring and demolishing everything in its path.
It rests,
Weaving a shell of silk,
Sleeping and disappearing,
Leaving no trace,
Until that day when it emerges, changed forever . . .

The butterfly is a kite on a gentle breeze,
Like a fairy dancing in the sunlight.
Flittering and fluttering,
Stately and imperial.
A confusion of colours, brilliant blues, ruby-reds,
Gracious greens, powerful pinks, princely purples
And youthful yellows.
Delicate, elegant and graceful,
She glides from flower to flower,
Ever searching for her sweet kiss of nectar,
Her lifeblood and spirit.

Eleanor Dudley (10)
Woodlea Primary School

Dinosaurs

As the sun rises
A distinguished carnotaurus roars in the sunlight

A vicious tyrannosaurus rex roars in victory in front of its prey.

Pterosaurs flying
In the mists of fish
Swooping
Down, down, down
Into the sparkling river.

Deinosuchus
Is here too
But he is not after fish
He is after the pterosaurs.

He jumps out of the water
And catches the
Pterosaurs
And gorges it immediately.

As the sun sets
A
Terrifying allosaurus
Screeches as the sunset
Makes its move.

Alexander Summers (8)
Woodlea Primary School

The Plastic Bag

The plastic bag,
The plastic bag,
Oh what was in the plastic bag?
My mum told me not to look,
But that plastic bag had to be took.
Was it chocolate? Was it sweets?
Or could it be filled with lovely treats?
Oh reader, be quiet and let me think,
If I shook it would it clink?
Would it bang?
Would it clang?
Maybe shaking isn't a good idea,
It could break, that's what I fear.
Shall I look? Oh dear, oh dear,
Shall I just have a peep?
All I'd have to do is creep.
The temptation is driving me crazy!
My eyesight is going a little bit hazy.
So that's why I'm sneaking,
Towards my prize,
And what do I find to my surprise?
Now listen, this is what I have to say,
It was an Action Man for my brother's birthday!

Madelyn Harper (10)
Woodlea Primary School

Scuba Diving

The most wonderful feeling in the world
Is to dive into the
Majestic ocean
To be surrounded by
Exotic
Multicoloured
Fish.
It is like a
Rainbow
Of gleaming
Scales
The colours are
Amazing.
Shimmering silver
Toffee brown
Coal black
Fire red
Purple like robes of a Roman
Emperor.
As you find out you have to leave
A wave of disappointment showers you
But you always have the memories of your first
Scuba dive.

Jessica Weetman (8)
Woodlea Primary School

Seasons

In the spring
I smelt the blossom
I felt the trees
I heard the birds
I felt happy

In the summer
I smelt the air
I heard the bees
I touched the flowers
I felt calm

In the autumn
I felt the pine cones
I crunched the leaves
I collected the conkers
I felt relaxed

In the winter
I felt the snow
I smelt the pine
I saw the Christmas tree
I felt excited.

Seasons are *great!*

Leah Cain (10)
Woodlea Primary School

My Sister, Mandy

I woke up feeling fine and dandy
But then I thought of my sister, Mandy
She stinks like compost and rotten candy
I'd just calmed down when I saw . . .

My brother, Shane
I think he belongs down the drain
He's a terrible show-off, yes he is
He knows everything that's not his biz
I'd just calmed down when I thought of . . .

My stepdad, Jim
He belongs in the bin
All he does is drink gin
Which I say is a sin
I'd just calmed down when I remembered . . .

It was time to go to school . . .
Oh school, school, terrible school
All you do is listen to rules
Today was the worst I don't know why
Oh why aren't I able to fly?
I'd just got there when I realised
It was *Saturday!*

Elise Miller (10)
Woodlea Primary School

I'm Not Frightened

Night is dark,
Night is scary,
But it doesn't frighten me.
Ghosts are frightening,
A very rare sighting,
But it doesn't frighten me.
Monsters under my bed,
Shadows on the shed,
It doesn't frighten me.
Beasts beneath the stairs,
It doesn't give me nightmares,
So it still doesn't frighten me!
Faces on the moon,
Or a huge typhoon,
It doesn't frighten me.
Crashes and bangs in the dark,
Or a great white shark,
It doesn't frighten me.
But when I'm lying in my bed,
And the door slowly opens,
My legs go wobbly, my teeth chatter,
And now I feel frightened!

Elizabeth Lewis-Orr (9)
Woodlea Primary School

Dinosaurs Fight

As the sun rose over the mountains,
A majestic ankylosaurus
Awakens the herd,
However,
A raptor cries
Loudly,
And the fight began.

The stegosaurus fought hard,
Whirling,
Slamming
Their tails.
Triceratops charging,
Ramming their horns.
Ultrasaur crushing with his legs.

As the sun set over the valley,
The carnivores beat a hasty
Retreat.
The herbivores had won
The mighty battle,
So peace returned to the valley
Once again.

Andrew Gurr (9)
Woodlea Primary School

Untitled

It's winter now, summer has passed by,
There's no time to fly delightful kites
Whilst birds are gliding high.

It's winter now, summer has passed by,
I run outside in my puffy, pink boots
To find the crystal-white snow.
The kerb covered up,
White crystal flakes land on my face
While soft winds blow.

It's winter now, summer's passed by,
I hopped up from my pancake shape,
Sprinting up over the kerb,
White crystal flakes all over my face,
Running over at a break-neck pace.

It's winter now, summer passed by,
It's getting cold, I'm feeling cold,
My blood frozen inside me.
I run inside,
I sit by the autumn-orange flames
With a cup of tea beside me.

Abigail Roffey (10)
Woodlea Primary School

Firework Night

Crackle!
Bang!
Firework night has started.
Sapphire-blue,
Toffee-brown,
Ruby-red,
Snow-white,
Plum-purple,
Banana-yellow,
They will hypnotise you.
The bonfire flames dance like
Golden serpents
In the pitch-black night sky.
Excited children wrap up warm
In their winter woollies and their waterproof wellies.
Sticky toffee apples,
Steaming hot dogs,
Pink candyfloss like sticky, sweet clouds.
Crackle!
Bang!
Firework night has started.

Eleanor Haysom (8)
Woodlea Primary School

Paper

Paper, Can be a drawing,
Can be a book,
Can be a poem,
Can be a diary,
Can be my homework,
Can turn fiery,
Can be a picture,
Can be a map,
Can be a letter,
Can be a contract,
Can be an aeroplane,
Can be a painting,
Can be a plan,
Can be the news,
Can be shredded,
Can be recycled,
Can be maché,
Can be origami,
Is this what a seed of a tree
Thinks it can be?

Leo Bennett (9)
Woodlea Primary School

Pets

Loving, energetic dogs rolling in the sun.
Tiny ones, huge ones, bulky ones,
And ones just right for you.

Funny, multicoloured dogs playing in a field.
Some barking, some whining,
Also some just chilling out.

Cuddly, cute dogs lying in their beds,
Long hair, short hair,
Plus some with curly fur too.

Colourful, bouncy dogs all in a huddle,
Toffee-brown, dark black, blonde-white, light grey
And some in a muddle.

Tired, beautiful dogs sleeping on the floor,
Making all sorts of noises,
Running, barking
In their sleep,
Making me
Giggle!

Oliver Sullivan (9)
Woodlea Primary School

Firework Night

I walk into a park on a jet-black night.
Suddenly a
Crackle!
Pop!
Snap!
Boom!
Lights up the sky.
A ruby-red hypnotising Catherine wheel
Whizzes round on its stick
As tall as the bonfire.

The burning wood smell fills the air
Smells of mouth-watering hot dogs drift past my nose
I eat some sticky, pink strawberry candyfloss
That sticks to my chin
There is a popcorn stall where you can buy
Toffee popcorn
Sweet popcorn, salty popcorn
I choose the delicious toffee popcorn.
Yummy!

Faye Baker (8)
Woodlea Primary School

Winter

A blanket of snow fell in the night,
As pure white as can be,
Sparkling under the delicate sun,
Shining under starlit sky,
Lying silently on the ground.

Lacy snowflakes floating gently to the ground,
As robins create tiny tracks leading to another world,
As the sun starts to shine,
The blanket of snow fades away,
The wonderful season is over.

Eloise Marchant (9)
Woodlea Primary School

My Dream World

In my dreams,
I dream of a world,
A world where things are my own,
Where people are always smiling - smiling with happiness.

In my dreams,
I dream of a world,
A world where things are my own,
Where the imaginary animals are blessed with joy.

In my dreams,
I dream of a world,
A world where things are my own,
Where the wonderful smell of pure fresh air is all around you.

In my dreams,
I dream of a world,
A world where things are my own,
Where everything is in its place,
And everything revolves perfectly around me.

Amber Hill (10)
Woodlea Primary School

Firework Night

Crackle! Bang!
Firework night has come
Sizzle! Pop!
There goes the first firework as it lights up the sky.
Crackle! Whoo!
A Catherine wheel has just started, what a fabulous sight!
I can see a rainbow of colours: violet, indigo, azure-blue, emerald-green.
Sizzle! Pop!
We all crowd round the hot dog stall waiting for our food.
What a great evening!

Olivia Barwick (9)
Woodlea Primary School

Jealousy

Jealousy is the colour of the great big bang,
Jealousy looks like a blood-sucking fang,
Jealousy tastes like a horrid payback,
Jealousy feels like an old, old shack,
Jealousy sounds like hard work, puff, puff, puff,
We all hate jealousy, so stop . . .

Enough!

Emma Vivian (8)
Worplesdon Primary School

Happiness

Happiness is the colour of people splashing in the blue sea
Happiness smells like delicious food
Happiness sounds like waves whooshing in the sea
Happiness is like tasting munchy chicken
Happiness looks like the bright, golden sun
Happiness feels like the sand on a beach
Happiness reminds me of having a party with my family.

Eliot Glaysher (8)
Worplesdon Primary School

Happiness

Happiness is the colour of rosy pink
Happiness looks like a heart of ink
Happiness smells like steamy chips
Happiness tastes like warm specks on your lips
Happiness sounds like a gentle flute
Happiness feels like a nice warm toot
Happiness reminds me of a nice flower's root.

Emily Jane Ofield (8)
Worplesdon Primary School

Pain

Pain is the colour of blood dripping red
Pain sounds like a lion roaring in bed
Pain tastes like bitter blood being fed
Pain looks like someone lying dead
Pain reminds me of someone in a hospital bed
Pain feels like a sword going through your head
Pain smells like a rotting, raging ted.

Katie Barnes (9)
Worplesdon Primary School

Anger

Anger is the colour of ruby-red,
Anger feels like sharp, sharp lead,
Anger sounds like waves against the rocks,
Anger looks like a fearsome fox,
Anger tastes like ashes from a fire,
I hate anger, it makes me tire!

Shannon White (8)
Worplesdon Primary School

Courage

Courage is as solid as rocks being crushed
Courage is as salty as the deep, aqua sea
Courage smells like ash burning red
Courage sounds as loud as thunder
Courage is the colour of burning flames
Courage is the look on a proud, bold lion.

Luke Green (8)
Worplesdon Primary School

Silence

Silence is the colour of milky-white
Silence smells like minty air floating around
Silence looks like a clear, silent night
Silence tastes like melting marshmallows
Silence reminds me of an abandoned beach
Where all you can hear is the crashing of the waves.

Erin Alesbury (8)
Worplesdon Primary School

Jealousy

Jealousy is enough to make you bite your lip.
Jealousy sounds like a jammed, stuck zip.
Jealousy is the colour of a green, brown bog.
Jealousy looks like a fierce dog.
Jealousy feels like spiky, tough metal
And looks like a big, gory battle.

Daisy Edwards (8)
Worplesdon Primary School

Pain

Pain is the colour of burning fear
Pain is the feeling of blame
Pain is the beginning of fear
Pain is the opposite to a loving deer
Pain is something that everybody fears
Yes, yes, yes, so stop right here!

Nikhil Woodruff (8)
Worplesdon Primary School

Anger

Anger is the colour of horrible black,
Anger tastes like salt on a crack.
Anger sounds like shouting in the night,
Anger tastes like salt on a light.
Anger looks like fire on a hill,
Anger feels like someone being killed.

Charlie Gregory (8)
Worplesdon Primary School

Happiness

Happiness smells like blossom falling from the tree,
Happiness is the colour of the light blue sea,
Happiness is yummy and sweet, it tastes like me,
Happiness sounds like children laughing,
Happiness feels like a new friend dancing.

Mia Spanswick (8)
Worplesdon Primary School

Young Writers Information

We hope you have enjoyed reading this book - and that you will continue to enjoy it in the coming years.

If you like reading and writing poetry drop us a line, or give us a call, and we'll send you a free information pack.

Alternatively if you would like to order further copies of this book or any of our other titles, then please give us a call or log onto our website at www.youngwriters.co.uk.

Young Writers Information
Remus House
Coltsfoot Drive
Peterborough
PE2 9JX
(01733) 890066